A NEW GENERATION OF EVIDENCE

The Family Is Critical to Student Achievement

Edited by Anne T. Henderson and Nancy Berla

Second Printing 1995, Third Printing 1996, Fourth Printing 1997
Center for Law and Education
1875 Connecticut Ave., NW, Suite 510
Washington, DC 20009
202-462-7688

Originally published by
National Committee for Citizens in Education
Copyright 1994

ISBN 0-934460-41-8

Library of Congress Catalog Number 94-65434

Printed in U.S.A.

Support for this project was generously provided by the Charles Stewart Mott Foundation
and the Danforth Foundation. The interpretations and conclusions in this report represent
the views of the authors and the National Committee for Citizens in Education and not
necessarily those of the Mott and Danforth Foundations, their trustees, or officers.

Dedication

This book is dedicated to J. William (otherwise Bill) Rioux, a founder of the National Committee for Citizens in Education, and the first and most insistent champion of the *Evidence* series.

Table of Contents

Foreword

New readers may not realize that this report is the third in the *Evidence* series. The first edition, *The Evidence Grows*, was published in 1981. At that time, it was not generally recognized that involving parents was important to improving student achievement. We found 35 studies, all positive, that documented significant, measurable benefits for children, families, and schools. The conclusion: "Taken together, what is most interesting about the research is that it all points in the same direction. The form of parent involvement does not seem to be critical, so long as it is reasonably well-planned, comprehensive and long-lasting."

By 1987, when *The Evidence Continues to Grow* was released, the subject had come into its own as a special topic of research. There were 15 new studies, in addition to the ones already covered in the first edition. Whole new areas were illuminated, such as Sandy Dornbusch's research on parenting styles, Reg Clark's study of high-achieving students from low-income Black families, James Coleman's analysis of the relationships between families and public versus parochial schools, and Rhoda Becher's work on successful practices of parent involvement.

Now, in 1994, the field has become a growth-industry. We found more studies than we could possibly include, many in whole new areas such as family literacy, the effects of changes in family status and structure on student achievement, and nationally disseminated programs to promote family-school partnerships. To identify studies, we did a search through ERIC (Educational Research Information Clearinghouse), called leading researchers in the field, including the Center on Families, Communities, Schools and Children's Learning, and contacted the national programs for evaluation reports.

In choosing which studies to include, we tried to cover the range without being exhaustive. There is, we hope, a balance by topic, approach, and age level, as well as a mix of longitudinal studies, research on effects of programs and other interventions, studies of family process and status variables, and of school and community settings. Two major areas of research, changes in family structure and status and their effect on student achievement, and the contributions of families to their children's general development, are covered by reviews by Ann Milne and Diane Scott-Jones.

In this report, we have covered 66 studies, reviews, reports, analyses and books. Of these, 39 are new; 27 have been carried over from the previous editions. While there are several new and interesting studies of school or community-based programs and interventions, the area that has generated the most new study is the family. Of the 29 studies on how family background and behaviors influence student achievement, only 5 were included in *The Evidence Continues to Grow*. These have added tremendously to our knowledge about the contributions families make to their children's success, and the supports families need from schools and community sources to guide their children successfully through the system. We also know much more about the difficulties families from diverse cultural backgrounds and with low income face when they must deal with schools that are designed for white, middle-class children.

We use the term "family" rather than "parents" for an important reason. In many communities, children are raised by adults who are not their parents, or by older siblings. For many, this provides an extended support system, and those who are responsible for the children and who function effectively as their family deserve recognition.

In keeping with NCCE's mission of putting the public back in the public schools, the purpose of this report is to make the research accessible to the general reader. As in the previous editions, we have tried to keep the language free of educational and research jargon. We have also focused far more on study design and findings than on statistical methodology. For those who want more technical detail, or who would like to read entire studies, we have included wherever possible the ERIC ED or EJ numbers (see "Notes to the Reader")

We hope that this latest, and last, addition to the series will find uses and readers we cannot even imagine, and that it will inform and inspire the many people who carry on at the front lines with such courage and dedication. To those who ask whether involving parents will really make a difference, we can safely say that the case is closed.

* Use family instead of "Parents"-

* Courage and Dedication.

I Carry on.
I am inspired because I carry on at the front lines
with courage & dedication.

What the Studies Cover

Programs and Interventions

Early Childhood/ Preschool

Bronfenbrenner
Cochran et al.
Cummins
Goodson & Hess
Gordon
Gotts
Guinagh & Gordon
Irvine
Lazar
Mowry
Olmsted & Rubin
Pfannensteil
Radin
Schweinhart et al.
Stearns & Peterson
White et al.

Elementary School

Armor
Beane
Becher
Comer
Comer & Haynes
Dauber & Epstein
Epstein
Gillum
Leler
Swap
Thompson
Tizard et al.
Toomey
Walberg et al.

High School

Chavkin
Nettles
Simich-Dudgeon

School Policies

Coleman & Hoffer
McDill
Phillips
Wagenaar

Family Processes

Family Behavior & Background

Benson et al.
Bloom
Caplan et al.
Clark/1983
Clark/1990
Clark/1993
Dornbusch et al.
Kellaghan et al.
Milne
Schiamberg et al.
Scott-Jones/1984
Scott-Jones/1987
Steinberg et al.
Wong Fillmore

Family Relations with School

Baker & Stevenson
Eagle
Fehrmann et al.
Goldenburg
Lareau
Melnick & Fiene
Mitrsomwang et al.
Reynolds
Reynolds et al.
Rumburger
Sattes
Snow et al.
Stevenson & Baker
Walberg
Ziegler

Acknowledgments

The *Evidence* series has a long history, to which many people have contributed. First, NCCE staff: In 1981, Stan Salett discovered a reference linking parent-teacher organizations to student achievement and wondered if there were other studies. Bill Rioux thought we should publish something about it if there were, then later insisted on two updates "before someone else does it for us." Chrissie Bamber designed all three publications, arranged for promotion, and patiently set new deadlines as the old ones went unmet. Susan Hlesciak Hall did a masterful job of editing this edition. Caroline Lander and Heather Gold were immensely helpful in tracking down and summarizing the studies.

Another special mention goes to Pat Edwards at the Charles Stewart Mott Foundation, who skillfully arranged for essential financial support to typeset and print both this edition and its predecessor. Her encouragement and support of this project and many others at NCCE over the years are deeply appreciated.

Kathryn Nelson and Janet Levy at the Danforth Foundation made possible the matching funds to cover research assistance and writing. We also turned to our colleagues in the research community: Joyce Epstein, who sent us her excellent study and gave us good advice; Reg Clark, who tipped us off to recent research and whose own work has made such a contribution; and Sandy Dornbusch, who shared his own recent work and that of his colleagues.

We would like to thank friends at Foundations who have provided long-term support for NCCE's work to promote parent and citizen involvement in public education: Peter Gerber at the John D. and Catherine T. MacArthur Foundation, Hayes Mizell at the Edna McConnell Clark Foundation, Gayle Dorman at Lilly Endowment (now at Mary Reynolds Babcock Foundation), Ed Meade at the Ford Foundation, and (again) Pat Edwards at the Mott Foundation. Their vision and guidance have been invaluable.

Our readers also gave us excellent advice: Oliver Moles at the Education Department and Dan Safran of the Center for the Study of Parent Involvement, who identified points that needed more discussion or justification; Norm Fruchter at the Aaron Diamond Foundation, who found the weak spots; and Don Davies of the Center on Families, Communities, Schools and Children's Learning, who helped frame the questions for further research and provided a splendid quote for the back cover.

The beautiful images appearing on the cover and throughout this report are by artist Bill Harris, who gave us permission to use "The Neighborhood," an original linoleum block print.

Finally, we would like to thank our families for their patience and cooperation. Mike Berla fielded phone calls and provided able technical assistance on the computer; Basil Henderson was a wonderful first reader; Amy-Louise Henderson graciously yielded time at the family computer. Looking at the piles of reports, drafts, disks, and other detritus accumulated in our offices and throughout the house, they concluded that the Evidence was Out of Control. Support from families is, of course, what this report is all about.

Notes to the Reader

Many of the studies covered in this bibliography are available through the Educational Resource Information Center (ERIC) System. If the citation includes a listing of "ED" or "EJ" followed by a six-digit number, reprints of the report, study or article are available, by calling the following organizations. You can order the documents by telephone, if they are charged on a credit card.

For ED numbers, CBIS
            7420 Fullerton Road, Suite 110
            Springfield, Virginia 22153
            1-800-443-ERIC; 1-703-440-1400

For EJ numbers, University Microfilms International (UMI)
            Article Clearinghouse
            P.O. Box 1346
            Ann Arbor, Michigan 48106
            1-800-732-0616; 1-313-761-4700

Introduction

The evidence is now beyond dispute. When schools work together with families to support learning, children tend to succeed not just in school, but throughout life. In fact, the most accurate predictor of a student's achievement in school is not income or social status, but the extent to which that student's family is able to:

1. Create a home environment that encourages learning
2. Express high (but not unrealistic) expectations for their children's achievement and future careers
3. Become involved in their children's education at school and in the community.

Taken together, the studies summarized in this report strongly suggest that when schools support families to develop these three conditions, children from low-income families and diverse cultural backgrounds approach the grades and test scores expected for middle-class children. They also are more likely to take advantage of a full range of educational opportunities after graduating from high school. Even with only one or two of these conditions in place, children do measurably better at school.

The studies have documented these benefits for students:

- Higher grades and test scores
- Better attendance and more homework done
- Fewer placements in special education
- More positive attitudes and behavior
- Higher graduation rates
- Greater enrollment in postsecondary education.

Families benefit, too. Parents develop more confidence in the school. The teachers they work with have higher opinions of them as parents and higher expectations of their children. As a result, parents develop more confidence not only about helping their children learn at home, but about themselves as parents. Furthermore, when parents become involved in their children's education, they often enroll in classes to continue their own education.

Schools and communities also profit. Schools that work well with families have:

- Improved teacher morale
- Higher ratings of teachers by parents
- More support from families
- Higher student achievement
- Better reputations in the community.

When parents are involved in their children's education at home, their children do better in school. When parents are involved at school, their children go farther in school, and the schools they go to become better.

The Studies

The research described in this report divides loosely into two categories:

1. Studies that evaluate or assess the effects of programs and other interventions

- Early childhood and preschool programs providing educational opportunities and home visits for families with infants and toddlers
- Programs to help elementary and middle schools work more closely with families
- Programs in high schools and community efforts to support families in providing wider opportunities for young people.

2. Studies that look at family processes -- the ways families behave and interact with their children

- The relationship between family background (e.g. income, education level, ethnicity) and student achievement
- Characteristics of home learning environments (e.g. monitoring homework, reading, eating meals together) and their effects on student performance
- Class and cultural "mismatch," or what happens when children's background does not match the expectations of schools.

Programs and Interventions

1. For Preschool Children

The most extensively documented form of intervention is parent education for families with young children, whether through home visits and nearby group meetings, or as part of a preschool program such as Head Start. If the program is well-designed, the effects on children can be measured many years later.

This chart, from the Schweinhart and Weickart study of the Perry Preschool Program in Ypsilanti, Michigan, presents some of the striking results they documented. It compares two groups of 19-year-olds: those who participated in the program at ages two to four, and those from a matched control group who did not participate:

Outcome at Age 19	Perry Preschool	No Preschool
High School Graduates	67%	49%
Employed	50%	32%
On Welfare	18%	32%
Ever Arrested	31%	51%

This rigorous long-term study was done on a high-quality preschool program that met two-and-a-half hours a day, twice a week for two years, with well-designed and extensive parent education and outreach. Edward Gotts' thorough study of HOPE (Home-Oriented Preschool Education), a much less intensive preschool program in rural Appalachia, which was delivered through television, weekly sessions held in mobile classrooms, and home visits once a week, also shows improved attendance, higher grades, and improved scores on tests of achievement and ability over the long term.

Programs that teach mothers to use learning materials at home and support them with home visits about once a week also have effects that last well into elementary school. (Bronfenbrenner, Guinagh and Gordon) These appear to be more effective than formal preschool programs with low parent involvement. (Bronfenbrenner, Mowry) Irving Lazar's longer-term study of students who graduated from Head Start programs with high parent involvement found positive effects through high school.

As Bronfenbrenner says, "to use a chemical analogy, parent intervention functions as a kind of *fixative*, which stabilizes effects produced by other processes." In their review of research on the home environment and school learning, Kellaghan and his colleagues conclude, "today, many commentators would view any attempt at intervention with children from disadvantaged backgrounds that did not include a home component as unlikely to be very effective." (p.13)

The one study that does not concur was done by Karl White and others at Utah State University. Their analysis of 193 studies of programs for disadvantaged and handicapped children found few that met their standards of methodological validity and concluded that the evidence of benefits for children is not convincing. Because the studies in this field were done by a wide variety of researchers with many different perspectives, it seems unrealistic to expect their work to have conformed to the set of extremely rigorous standards that White and his colleagues propose. Taken together, the studies summarized in this report do make a strong case, although additional, more rigorously designed research would certainly be welcome.

> "Today, many commentators would view any attempt at intervention with children from disadvantaged backgrounds that did not include a home component as unlikely to be very effective."

2. In Elementary and Middle Schools

. Begin to grow or increase rapidly (develop quickly)
. Flourish
Burgeon —

Over the past ten years, the number of programs and other organized efforts by schools to reach out and engage parents in their children's education has burgeoned. Not only are local, home-grown programs such as Indianapolis Parents in Touch becoming widely known and imitated, but nationally disseminated programs such as the Quality Education Program, Family Math and Family Science, MegaSkills, Parents as Teachers, and James Comer's School Development Program, are being widely adopted.

To make sense of this sometimes bewildering array, Susan Swap has developed a helpful four-part typology of home-school relationships. Her first two types, the "protective model" (where schools enforce strict separation between parents and educators) and the "school to home transmission model" (where teachers send one-way communications), are common practice. The second two, "curriculum enrichment" and "partnership" are coming into wider use.

In the "curriculum enrichment" model, parents contribute their knowledge and skills to the school. Parents explain their cultural heritage as part of a multicultural program, for example, or help to set up a science learning center, or collaborate with teachers to reinforce at home what is being taught at school. Several studies document positive effects of this approach, particularly in reading. (Dauber and Epstein, Epstein, Tizard et al.)

> Parents are much more likely to become involved when teachers encourage and assist parents to help their children with schoolwork.

Epstein carefully tracks the importance of teacher leadership. Parents are much more likely to become involved when teachers encourage and assist parents to help their children with schoolwork. A number of other studies reinforce her additional point that teachers have higher expectations of students whose parents collaborate with them; they also have higher opinions of those parents. (Lareau, Snow et al., Stevenson and Baker) Conversely, parents who become involved are more satisfied with schools and hold their children's teachers in higher regard. (Dauber and Epstein, Epstein, Melnick and Fiene, Phillips) Although the causal path is not always clear, the relationship between these efforts and an improvement in student achievement is well-documented.

In his study of low-income elementary schools in Australia, Derek Toomey found an interesting counter-effect. Programs offering home visits were more successful in involving low-income parents than were programs requiring parents to visit the school, but when parents chose the school visit program, their children made greater gains. These parents became an "in-group," discouraging the families who were more comfortable at home. Toomey speculates that teachers favor parents who are willing to come to school, and the parents who do come are more self-confident and committed to the program.

In Swap's "partnership" model, family members work alongside teachers on the common mission of helping all children to learn. Unlike the curriculum enrichment strategy, where they are confined to certain settings, parents are involved in all aspects of school life. They volunteer in the classroom, tutor students, serve on committees, and establish contact with community groups. For most schools, this degree of partnership entails a transformation of their relationship with families.

This approach is exemplified by the School Development Program (SDP), which was developed by psychologist James Comer and his colleagues at the Yale Child Study Center. Their 15-year collaboration with two low-achieving elementary schools in New Haven has been quite successful. After 5 years both schools had the best attendance record in the city and near grade-level academic performance. After 15 years, with no change in their socio-economic makeup, students were performing at grade level; and there had been no serious behavior problems at either school for more than a decade. (Comer) Other SDP sites, which include both elementary and middle schools, report similar results. (Comer and Haynes)

Less ambitious efforts also bring benefits. David Armor identified 20 Los Angeles elementary schools serving low-income, minority populations that had substantially improved reading achievement. Establishing a range of school-community interaction from low to high, he correlated improvements in reading achievement with levels of interaction and found a positive relationship for schools with predominantly African American students: the higher the level of parent involvement, the higher the students' scores. The relationship did not appear for Mexican-American students, which Armor attributed to the language barrier.

Several studies assessed the effects of the Parent Education Follow Through Program, a model developed by Ira Gordon and his associates to help Head Start graduates with the transition to school. In this program, parents play six roles he defined as critical: classroom volunteer, paraprofessional, teacher at home, adult educator, adult learner, and decision maker. Gordon found that children showed the greatest gains when parents played all six roles. Other studies confirmed this; children in the program showed significant gains in reading achievement but gains in math tended to appear only when home visits were included. (Leler, Olmsted and Rubin; also see Epstein)

Teachers have higher expectations of students whose parents collaborate with them; they also have higher opinions of those parents.

In her review of parent education programs, Hazel Leler describes studies on a partnership-style bilingual Follow Through program, where students performed up to two times the levels of matched comparison groups, then approached or surpassed national norms after one or two years.

Although new and yet to be extensively evaluated, the Quality Education Program (QEP) seems to be having a positive effect on elementary school students' test scores. At the end of one year, QEP districts in Mississippi averaged a 4.8 percent increase in standardized test scores, compared to an increase of only .3 percent in the control districts. In this program, parents attend seminars, receive coaching in home-school activities, and receive extensive communications from school. Teachers and administrators also receive training in how to collaborate with families. (Thompson)

3. In High Schools and the Community

Improving student achievement by working more closely with families appears to be used as a strategy most often in preschool and elementary school. Only two of the studies discussed above included middle school students (Comer and Haynes, Dauber and Epstein), and only three of the 34 studies that look at programs or other interventions are addressed to the high school level. There is, however, some evidence that such a strategy is equally effective with older students. The following chart from Eva Eagle's study shows that high school graduates with parents who were "highly involved" during the high school years were much more likely to complete a 4-year college education:

Students' highest level of Education:	Parents Highly Involved During HS	Parents Moderately Involved During HS	Parents Not Very Involved During HS
BA or BS degree	27%	17%	8%
Some Post-Sec Ed	53	51	48
HS Diploma	20	32	43

The Trinity-Arlington Project described by Carmen Simich-Dudgeon was designed to increase the participation of high school students' families from four different language groups, Spanish, Vietnamese, Khmer, and Lao. Teachers were trained in techniques for involving parents, and parents were trained in how to guide their children through high school and vocational opportunities. Students' scores in English proficiency increased significantly.

Two other studies looked at results of family-school-community collaborations. In San Marcos, Texas, a school of social work at a local university formed a coalition with the school district and community groups to support an alternative high school for actual and potential dropouts. Although long-term data are not yet available, Chavkin describes dramatic benefits from casework with individual students and families. Saundra Nettles's interesting study of thirteen community-based interventions for low-income high school students found positive effects for students, not only in grades and attendance, but also in reduced risk-taking behavior.

*   *   *

Across the programs studied, student achievement increased directly with the duration and intensity of parent involvement. Fifteen studies established increments or levels of involvement (as opposed to just comparing students in programs that include parent involvement with students in a control group, or with a pre-program baseline). Each one reported that the more parents are involved, the better students perform in school. (Armor, Bronfenbrenner, Eagle, Gillum, Gordon, Gotts, Irvine, Leler, McDill, Mitrsomwang and Hawley, Mowry, Phillips, Radin, Toomey, Wagenaar, Walberg et al.)

Some researchers have taken the reverse perspective, by looking at whether schools with high average achievement have more parent and community involvement than similar schools with low achievement. In an important 1969 nationwide study, McDill concluded that the degree of parent and community interest in quality education is "the critical factor in explaining the impact of the high school environment on the achievement and educational aspirations of students."(p. 27) A study of elementary schools in a large midwestern city eight years later found that schools with high achievement levels are more open to parent and community involvement. (Wagenaar) In 1985, a study commission in Milwaukee found that parent involvement is associated with higher school performance regardless of family income, grade level, or type of neighborhood. (Phillips et al.)

> In fact, it appears that the more programs take on a "partnership" relationship with families, the more successful they are in raising student achievement to national norms. Why should we be satisfied with less?

Coleman and Hoffer, exploring why inner-city Catholic schools produce students who are more successful than comparable students in public schools, attribute the disparity to the different relationship the schools have to their communities. Public schools perceive themselves as an instrument of society designed to help children overcome the deficiencies of their families. Parochial schools see themselves as extensions not of the social order, but of the families they serve. This continuity of values and mutual support reinforces the children's educational experiences and relieves the cultural mismatch identified in other studies. In other words, what is important is not the type of school, or who goes there, but the quality of its relationship with the families it serves.

This display of steady improvement raises an important equity issue, which Swap refers to as "the ceiling effect." Although parent involvement is consistently effective in raising low-income students' grades and test scores, many programs are considered successful even if the improved achievement is still well below grade level. Several studies strongly suggest that programs designed with extensive parent involvement can boost low-income students' achievement to levels expected for middle-class students. In fact, it appears that the more programs take on a "partnership" relationship with families, the more successful they are in raising student achievement to national norms. (Cochran and Henderson, Comer, Comer and Haynes, Leler, Swap, Tizard et al.) Why should we be satisfied with less?

Family Processes

The second group of studies examines the relationship between parent involvement and student achievement from the family perspective, by assessing how family background and behavior influence children's development. Directly or indirectly, all the studies address the extent to which family socio-economic status (SES) determines the quality of student performance. SES consists of a cluster of variables such as mother's education, family income, and father's occupational status.

1. Family Background and Student Achievement

When we look only at the relationship between SES and student achievement, we see a strong positive correlation. Children's grades, test scores, graduation rates, and enrollment in post-secondary education tend to increase with each level of education that their mothers have completed. (Baker and Stevenson, Benson et al., Eagle, Sattes) The real question, of course, is *why*? Sattes responds succinctly: "The fact that family SES is related to school achievement doesn't mean that rich kids are born smarter. It means that, in more affluent families, children are more likely to be exposed to experiences that stimulate intellectual development." (p.2)

Eva Eagle's study adroitly peels apart these layers. Using the data base from a large national study of high school students, she found that "students' educational attainment was strongly associated with all five indicators in the SES composite." (p.3) In this study, SES was defined as mother's education, father's education, family income, father's occupational status, and number of major possessions (e.g. cars, appliances).

Next, Eagle identified the family characteristics that are most associated with achievement in families of all SES levels. She found that parents of good students provide a quiet place to study, emphasize family reading, and stay involved in their children's education.

Having established that both high SES and certain family practices are associated with student achievement, Eagle asked whether family practices can have an effect independent of SES. That is, can all families help their children progress to higher education by monitoring their schoolwork, helping develop post-high school plans, and staying in touch with their teachers? Eagle found that those most likely to enroll in and complete post-secondary education were the ones whose parents were highly involved in their education, regardless of SES.

In her paper, Suzanne Ziegler concluded that parent encouragement at home and participation in school activities are the key factors related to children's achievement, more significant than either student ability or SES. Ann Milne's extensive review of over 100 studies covering not only SES, but also family structure and mothers' employment outside the home, drew an even broader conclusion: "what is important is the ability of the parent(s) to provide proeducational resources for their children -- be they financial, material, or experiential." (p.58)

Kellaghan, Sloane, Alvarez, and Bloom, in their book *Home Environment and School Learning*, summarize this way:

> The socio-economic level or cultural background of a home need not determine how well a child does at school.

> *Eagle found that those most likely to enroll in and complete post-secondary education were the ones whose parents were highly involved in their education, regardless of SES.*

[handwritten margin note: "it's what parents do at home"]

Parents from a variety of cultural backgrounds and with different levels of education, income or occupational status can and do provide stimulating home environments that support and encourage the learning of their children. It is what parents do in the home rather than their status that is important. (p.145)

2. Families as Learning Environments

Another group of studies looked at the types of family interactions and behavior associated with high-achieving students, and compared them to families with low-achieving students. As Reginald Clark points out in his 1990 article subtitled "What Happens Outside School Is Critical," students spend about 70 percent of their waking hours outside of school. The way that time is spent can have a powerful influence on what and how much children learn.

The descriptions of families whose children who are doing well in school repeatedly mention these characteristics and examples:[1]

◆ **Establishing a daily family routine** -- providing time and a quiet place to study, assigning responsibility for household chores, being firm about times to get up and go to bed, having dinner together. (Benson et al., Clark/1983, Eagle, Kellaghan et al., Walberg et al.)

◆ **Monitoring out-of-school activities** -- setting limits on tv watching, checking up on children when parents are not home, arranging for after-school activities and supervised care. (Benson et al., Clark/1990, Walberg)

◆ **Modeling the value of learning, self-discipline, and hard work** -- communicating through questioning and conversation, demonstrating that achievement comes from working hard, using reference materials and the library. (Caplan et al., Clark/1993, Dornbusch et al., Rumburger et al., Snow et al., Steinburg et al.)

◆ **Expressing high but realistic expectations for achievement** -- setting goals and standards that are appropriate for children's age and maturity, recognizing and encouraging special talents, informing friends and family about successes. (Bloom, Kellaghan et al., Reynolds et al., Schiamberg and Chun, Scott-Jones/1984, Snow et al.)

◆ **Encouraging children's development and progress in school** -- maintaining a warm and supportive home, showing interest in children's progress at school, helping with homework, discussing the value of a good education and possible career options, staying in touch with teachers and school staff. (Baker and Stevenson, Dauber and Epstein, Eagle, Kellaghan et al., Fehrmann et al., Melnick and Fiene, Mitrsomwang and Hawley, Stevenson and Baker, Snow et al., Ziegler)

◆ **Reading, writing and discussions among family members** -- reading, listening to children read, and talking about what is being read; discussing the day over dinner; telling stories and sharing problems; writing letters, lists, and messages. (Becher, Epstein, Kellaghan et al., Scott-Jones/1987, Snow et al., Tizard et al., Ziegler)

◆ **Using community resources for family needs** -- enrolling in sports programs or lessons, introducing children to role models and mentors, using community services. (Beane, Benson et al., Chavkin, Clark/1990, Nettles)

3. Class and Cultural "Mismatch"

Although parenting styles that produce high achievement can be found in families from all backgrounds, better performance is still strongly associated with more education and greater income. Low-SES students whose parents provide a strong home learning environment and stay involved with school still do not do as well in school as high-SES students from similar home environments. (Eagle. Also see Benson et al.)

> *When parents and schools collaborate to help children adjust to the world of school, bridging the gap between the culture at home and the mainstream American school, children of all backgrounds tend to do well.*

Annette Lareau examined the effects of social class differences on how White families relate to schools and support their children's learning. Comparing two schools, one in a college-educated, middle-class community, the other in a blue-collar, working-class neighborhood, Lareau found striking contrasts. Not only did middle-class families have the time, money and resources to be active partners with the school, their education enabled them to be more comfortable dealing with teachers. The working class parents, who had equally strong feelings about the importance of education, had to make complicated arrangements for transportation and childcare in order to attend meetings at school. When they arrived, their encounters with teachers were awkward and unproductive.

According to Lareau, middle-class culture and social networks build connections between home and school, reinforcing teachers' positive attitudes. Working class culture emphasizes separation between home and school, reducing the opportunities for collaboration and lowering teachers' expectations for children. As Lily Wong Fillmore puts it, the relationship between the middle-class home and school is a "seamless splice." Because schools play an important role in the process of reproducing the divisions in society, they sort students from different classes into categories that can sharply restrict their future opportunities. (Baker and Stevenson, Lareau, Snow et al.)

The differences in how families relate to school are rooted not only in class divisions, but also in ethnic diversity. In her review of research on families with different cultural and language backgrounds, Lily Wong Fillmore finds a profound "mismatch" between how low-income and minority children are raised and the background children require to prosper in American schools.

Wong Fillmore suggests that children from "mainstream" and Chinese-American families earn higher grades and test scores because the middle-class values and ways of learning promoted at home match those at school. Working-class Black and White children, and Mexican-Americans tend not to perform as well, because their families have emphasized good behavior, not literacy; because they are taught to learn by observation and imitation, not by direct instruction; and because their parents have encouraged an individual pace of development rather than pushing them to keep up with other children.

When parents and schools collaborate to help children adjust to the world of school, bridging the gap between the culture at home and the mainstream American school, children of all backgrounds tend to do well. As James Comer points out, "children learn from people they bond to." If children know that their parents and teachers understand and respect each other, that they share similar expectations and stay in touch, children feel comfortable with who they are and can more easily reconcile their experiences at home and school.

Claude Goldenburg's case studies of low-income Hispanic parents provide a telling example. "Freddy" was falling way behind in class when his first-grade teacher called his parents in to meet with her. Freddy's father and mother both came the next morning, and that afternoon, he got every word right on his spelling test. Every day after that, his mother came to school during reading hour. According to his teacher, "It's a whole new Freddy."

This research on family processes reveals that the home environment has a powerful influence not only on how well children do, but also on how far they go in school. If the family's approach to life and learning is very different from that of the school, children have difficulty integrating the two experiences and may drop out. On the other hand, cultural or socio-economic background does not rigidly determine a child's fate. What parents do at home to support learning has a strong, independent effect on children's achievement. But parents are in a much better position to assist their children if they are kept informed about how they are doing in school and the best ways to encourage them. (Kellaghan et al.)

> When they are treated as partners and given good information by people with whom they are comfortable, parents put into practice the strategies they already know are effective, but have not had the confidence or experience yet to attempt.

Doug Powell has reviewed some classic studies on educational attainment among working class youth.[2] The studies identified two types of families, "getting by" and "getting ahead." In "getting by" families, their way of life seemed preferable to the competitive game of rising higher, and children were encouraged to finish high school but not to attend college. In "getting ahead" families, parents stressed high marks, paid attention to what was happening at school, and suggested options for post-secondary education and future occupation.

Many of the studies reviewed here strongly suggest that when schools or community groups provide support, advice, and encouragement, lower-income families will adopt the "getting ahead" position with their children. (e.g. Beane, Becher, Cochran and Henderson, Comer, Epstein, Gillum, Gotts, Leler, Mitrsomwang and Hawley, Reynolds, Simich-Dudgeon, Walberg et al.) This is not to say that families should be taught how to be "better parents," or be lectured to about how to educate their children. When they are treated as partners and given good information by people with whom they are comfortable, parents put into practice the strategies they already know are effective, but have not had the confidence or experience yet to attempt.

Summing Up

A Caution

There are dangers in putting together a book like this. First, some may interpret the research on family processes to mean that families are -- and must be -- largely responsible for their children's achievement. We often hear comments like these: "Schools can only do so much, and they are already overburdened. Look at Asian families -- they raise children who take top honors, despite the hardships and disadvantages they have endured. Why can't other American families succeed in bootstrapping themselves as well?"

The response is that many can -- if they are given enough information, encouragement and support from schools and community services. Although the press is full of stories about the remarkable achievements of Asian families (Caplan et al.), their children often do no better in school than children of other minorities. In their study of Southeast Asian high school students, Mitrsomwang and Hawley found that families needed to provide three supports before their children performed above average at school.

- Hold strong, consistent values about the importance of education
- Be willing to help children with schoolwork and be in contact with the school
- Be **able** to help children with schoolwork and communicate successfully with teachers and administrators.

Baker and Stevenson reached similar conclusions in their study comparing middle-class and working-class families. Only when parents were able to intervene at school were students consistently steered toward higher-level and college-preparatory courses. For parents who may not speak English, or who do not know how the system works, or who themselves experienced failure as students, this can be a difficult task.

Knowing more about the qualities of families whose children perform well in school does not relieve schools of their obligation to make extra efforts for children who are falling behind. To the contrary, this knowledge can enable schools to support families, to help them develop and maintain an environment that encourages learning, to keep them informed about their children's progress, and to help them manage their children's advancement through the system. Neither families nor schools can do the job alone.

A second danger is that some might think that a simple parent involvement initiative is all that is necessary to improve student performance. Although reaching out to families and helping them become more engaged in their children's education at home and school can have a powerful impact on student achievement, effective efforts must have these three qualities:

- **Comprehensive**: Reaching out to all families, not just those most easily contacted, and involving them in all major roles, from tutoring to governance (Gordon)
- **Well-planned**: Specific goals, clear communication about what is expected of all participants, training for both educators and parents (Becher)
- **Long-lasting**: A clear commitment to the long-term, not just to an immediate project. (Gordon)

As Don Davies points out, the school must take the initiative to reach out to parents who have not been involved, and devise a wide variety of ways for them to participate. This means sending adequately prepared staff to visit homes, holding meetings outside the school in less intimidating and more accessible places such as churches, laundromats, and community gathering-places, preparing easy-to-read materials in different languages, and scheduling activities at times convenient for families. For families outside the mainstream, "a diverse and persistent strategy is needed to break down barriers and establish trust."[3]

Furthermore, involving parents will not compensate for a inadequate reading program, any more than public relations campaigns will cover up poor instruction and low expectations. Collaboration with families is an essential component of a reform strategy, but it is not a substitute for a high quality education program or thoughtful, comprehensive school improvement.

> *Collaboration with families is an essential component of a reform strategy, but it is not a substitute for a high quality education program or thoughtful, comprehensive school improvement.*

An Empowerment Model

In his provocative review, Jim Cummins proposes a framework for changing the relationship between families and schools, students and teachers, so that children from all groups in society have a better chance to succeed. Recent research by John Ogbu, an anthropologist, suggests that minority groups with low status tend to perform at a substandard level, because they have internalized the inferiority ascribed to them. For example, the Burakumin people do as poorly in Japanese schools as Blacks do in America. Yet when they attend school in the United States, they excel as often as other Asians.[4]

The central principle of Cummins' framework is that students from "dominated" minority groups can do well in school if they are empowered, rather than disabled, by their relationship with educators. According to Cummins, schools that empower their minority students have these characteristics:

- The students' language and culture are incorporated into the school program
- Family and community participation is an essential component of children's education
- Children are motivated to use language actively and to gain knowledge for their own use
- Educators serve as advocates for students rather than develop labels for students' "problems."

Major Findings

Throughout these studies, several themes emerged again and again:

◆ **First, the family makes critical contributions to student achievement, from earliest childhood through high school. Efforts to improve children's outcomes are much more effective if they encompass their families.**

Regardless of income, education level, or cultural background, all families can -- and do -- contribute to their children's success. When parents encourage learning and voice high expectations for the future, they are promoting attitudes that are keys to achievement. Students who feel that they have some control over their destiny, that they can earn an honorable place in society, that hard work will be recognized and rewarded, are students who do well in school. Although these attitudes are formed at home, they can be either strengthened or discouraged at school.

When schools encourage families to work with their children and provide helpful information and skills, they reinforce a positive cycle of development for both parents and students. The studies show that such intervention, whether based at home or at school, whether begun before or after a child enters school, has significant, long-lasting effects.

The reverse is also true. If schools disparage parents, or treat them as negative influences, or cut them out of their children's education, they promote attitudes in the family that inhibit achievement at school. Programs and policies to improve outcomes for students will be far more productive if they build on the strengths of families and enlist them as allies.

◆ **Second, when parents are involved at school, not just at home, children do better in school and they stay in school longer.**

Although the family learning environment makes important contributions to achievement, children still tend to fall behind if their parents do not participate in school events, develop a working relationship with their teachers, and keep up with what is happening at school.

Teachers hold higher expectations of students whose parents they see involved at school, and children whose parents are involved at the school have higher grades and test scores. This is especially true for students from low income and minority families.

In junior and senior high school, when the sorting and selection process intensifies, parents need to keep a careful watch over their children's placement. Students whose parents go to bat for them are more likely to take -- and pass -- higher level courses, and then to go on to college. High school students whose parents are not involved at school, on the other hand, are more likely to drop out.

Becoming involved at school has important effects not just for students, but for all members of the family. Parents develop more positive attitudes toward the school, become more active in community affairs, develop increased self-confidence, and enroll in other educational programs. This strengthens the family not only as a learning environment, but as an economic unit.

◆ **Third, when parents are involved at school, their children go to better schools.**

When parents are involved in different roles throughout the school, the performance of all children in the school tends to improve, not just the children of those who are actively involved. This may be because children whose families may not be active see parents just like their own having a positive impact. Successful program administrators, such as Genethia Hayes of Project AHEAD in the Los Angeles school district, estimate that when about one-third of parents in a school become actively involved, the school as a whole begins to turn around.

◆ **Fourth, children do best when their parents are enabled to play four key roles in their children's learning: teachers, supporters, advocates, and decision-makers.**

The studies describe four basic roles that parents play:

- As **teachers**, parents create a home environment that promotes learning, reinforces what is being taught at school, and develops the values and life skills children need to become responsible adults.
- As **supporters**, parents contribute their knowledge and skills to the school, enriching the curriculum, and providing extra services and support to students.
- As **advocates**, parents help children negotiate the system and receive fair treatment, and work to make the system more responsive to all families.
- As **decision-makers**, parents serve on advisory councils, curriculum committees, and management teams, participating in joint problem-solving at every level.

Most studies have focused on parents as teachers and supporters, roles that are customary to the early childhood and elementary school settings the programs address, and that have been more fully developed. In full partnerships, parents must be able to act as advocates and decision-makers as well.

Gotts attributes the lasting effects of the HOPE program to the fact that the parents became advocates, pushing the schools into offering better education and appraising school staff by how well they worked with parents. In the sobering epilogue to *Unfulfilled Expectations*, Snow and her colleagues describe what happened when working-class students entered secondary school. Only a few parents were able to deal the more complex school structure and continue to act as advocates for their children. As a result, most students in the study dropped out or were placed in the general or remedial programs.

> *The best results in Head Start and other parent education programs came when parents were involved in both learning and decision-making roles.*

The research is mixed on effects of parent involvement in decision-making. There is little evidence that putting parents on advisory councils or governing bodies improves their children's grades and test scores unless they are also involved in other ways. But when parents are given a role in governance as part of a comprehensive program, their children's achievement improves. The best results in Head Start and other parent education programs came when parents were involved in both learning and decision-making roles. (Gordon, Leler, Mowry) The four roles have a synergistic effect, each multiplying the influence of the others. Together they have a powerful impact.

◆ **Fifth, the more the relationship between family and school approaches a comprehensive, well-planned partnership, the higher the student achievement.**

Studies that correlate levels of parent involvement with increments in student achievement invariably find that the more extensive the involvement, the higher the student achievement. The specific form does not seem to be as important as the amount and variety of involvement.

In programs that are designed to be full partnerships, student achievement not only improves, it reaches levels that are standard for middle-class children. (Comer, Comer and Haynes, Cummins, Pfannensteil, Swap) And the children who are the farthest behind make the greatest gains. (Cochran and Henderson, Irvine)

Making the extra effort to engage families can have an important equalizing effect. By reversing the disabling, problem-oriented, divisive patterns of society, as Cummins suggests, schools can be transformed from places where only certain children can prosper into institutions where all children do well and are vitally connected to their communities.

◆ **Sixth, families, schools, and community organizations all contribute to student achievement; the best results come when all three work together.**

As Clark points out, the difference between high and low achieving youngsters may well be explained by how and with whom they spend their time outside school. Community organizations can provide important resources for both schools and families, and help establish a network of support for students after school and during vacations.

The work in many of the 90 schools that make up the League of Schools Reaching Out, which is sponsored by the Institute for Responsive Education, shows that it is possible for schools serving low-income families in communities plagued by terrible urban problems to establish and sustain working partnerships with their families, as well as with community agencies and organizations. This result challenges the assertion often made that family-school-community partnerships are fine in theory but can't be pulled off with disadvantaged families and in poor neighborhoods.[5]

More Questions to Address

The Center on Families, Communities, Schools and Children's Learning, sponsored by the U.S. Department of Education, is engaged in finding more specific answers to the questions of what interventions work under which conditions to foster children's academic and social development. To the Center and to other researchers in the United States and other countries whose work will add to the studies covered in this report, these additional questions may be helpful:

1. What strategies are most effective in raising the achievement level of low-income children to that expected for middle-class students?

2. What family factors and behaviors in different racial and ethnic groups contribute to children's academic success, across the age ranges from infancy through adolescence?

3. How can educators be better prepared to understand and address the critical role families and community organizations play in improving student outcomes?

4. How can schools be encouraged and supported to develop comprehensive and well-planned programs of partnership with families and community members?

5. What forms of family and community collaboration work best in middle and high schools? How can secondary schools be restructured to become more family-friendly and allow for more comprehensive parent participation?

6. What interventions by community agencies and organizations can support the learning and healthy development of children and youth? What are some effective processes for enabling families, schools and community organizations to collaborate on providing better conditions for kids to grow up and prosper?

7. What roles can children and youth play in these collaborations?

8. What policies -- federal, state, and local -- promote (or inhibit) the development of comprehensive and successful family-school-community partnerships?

Conclusion: Putting the Pieces Together

We don't know all we would like to know, but we certainly know more than enough to put in place a thoughtful, effective collaboration between schools and families, one that spans the full age range of schooling and that promises a serious improvement in student achievement and life prospects. These studies are like the pieces of a jigsaw puzzle; fitting them together gives us the whole picture.

When children are very young, they and their families benefit tremendously from programs that include home visits, where parents learn how to promote their children's growth and development. The lasting effects from such programs are documented well into the elementary grades.

During the preschool years, children who attend programs that foster their social and emotional development as well as intellectual skills, and that include home visits to their families to collaborate on the children's progress, are well prepared for school. This readiness is critical to their future success in school, and the positive effects of such programs can be tracked well into their graduates' early adulthood.

At elementary school, children whose families reinforce good work and study habits at home, emphasize the value of education, and express high expectations, tend to do well. They do even better if their parents come to school, stay informed about their progress, and collaborate with their teachers. Epstein's studies show this is much more likely to happen if teachers take the initiative, by encouraging and guiding parents in ways to help their children. For children from families considered "at-risk," who may be low-income or from cultural backgrounds different from the mainstream, a higher level of family-school collaboration may be required. The studies of partnership-style preschool and elementary programs show that chronic low achievement can be reversed in a few years.

The shift to middle or junior high school is difficult for most students and their families. When parents remain involved, their children make a better adjustment, keep up the quality of their work, and develop realistic plans for their future. Schools can help families with this transition. At a minimum, schools serving young adolescents should designate a teacher to serve as the parents' main contact, keep parents informed of all placement decisions and how they will affect the student's future options, and facilitate parent-to-parent contacts so that families can monitor their children's after-school and social activities. The few studies that look at parent involvement at the high school level reached similar findings. Students whose parents monitored their schoolwork and daily activities, talked frequently to their teachers, and helped develop their plans for education or work after high school, were much more likely to graduate and go on to post-secondary education.

*   *   *

The picture is coming into focus. The benefits of effective collaborations and how to do them are well documented across all the age ranges of schooling. Still they are not in widespread practice.

- The ultimate cost-savings of quality preschool programs that engage families are obvious -- yet they are available to less than half the children who would most benefit from them.

- Extra efforts to collaborate with families enable students to bond with the school and prosper academically -- yet how to collaborate with families is not covered in the curriculum of most teacher training institutions.

- Modest restructuring of middle and high schools could make it possible for teachers to work with smaller groups of students and collaborate more closely with their families -- yet most secondary schools are organized along factory lines the way they were 50 years ago.

- Community-wide collaborations to improve not only education but also the quality of life in the neighborhoods where children grow up can boost achievement and strengthen families -- yet most schools work in isolation from other community services.

Far too many families are poorly served by our chaotic, unresponsive, and inequitable educational system. Pervasively low test scores and high dropout rates, which in many cities approach 50 percent, degrade our workforce and signal a staggering waste of human potential. The urgent national reports that have chronicled these disorders in detail indeed present a picture of a nation at risk. If we are to be judged by how we treat our children, we face stern treatment.

The choice is ours. Is the mission of our public schools to reproduce the class divisions in society and perpetuate low achievement for the groups at the bottom of the social ladder? The unfortunate consequences of this practice are evident all around us.

Or is the mission of public education to enable all children to become healthy, happy, well-educated, and productive adults? The evidence presented is clear that we can do it, and there are many good examples of family, school and community partnership that point the way. More than grades and test scores are at stake. Central to our democracy is allowing parents and citizens to participate in the governing of public institutions and to have the deciding voice in how children are to be educated. Let us begin to work together to make it happen.

Footnotes

1. See Oliver Moles, ed., Schools and Families Together: Helping Children Learn More at Home. Workshops for Urban Educators. Commissioned by the Office of Educational Research and Improvement, U.S. Department of Education, March 1992. Workshop #1, "Families as Learning Environments," is organized around these characteristics.

2. Doug Powell, Literature Review, Department of Child Development and Family Studies, Purdue University, 1992.

3. Don Davies, "Parent Involvement in the Public Schools," in *Educational and Urban Society*, Vol. 19, No. 2, 1987, p. 157.

4. John Ogbu, "Understanding Cultural Diversity and Learning," a presentation to the American Educational Research Association, Chicago, March 1991.

5. Don Davies, Patricia Burch, and Vivian Johnson, " A Portrait of Schools Reaching Out: Report of a Survey of Practices and Policies of Family-Community-School Collaboration," Report #1, Center on Families, Communities, Schools and Children's Learning. (Baltimore: Johns Hopkins University, February 1992)

The Research Studies

Armor, David, and others   ED 130 243
"Analysis of the School Preferred Reading Program in Selected Los Angeles Minority Schools"
Rand Corporation, Santa Monica, CA, 1976

SUMMARY: A study of twenty elementary schools with predominantly low-income, minority student bodies, yet large or consistent gains in sixth-grade reading, found that the more vigorous the school's efforts to involve Black parents and community in all aspects of the school, the better the sixth-graders did in reading.

The researchers identified 20 schools in Los Angeles with substantial or consistent reading test score gains across sixth-grade classes between spring 1972 and fall 1975, enrollment of at least 490 students, and a ranking in the bottom half of family income levels. A balanced distribution between schools with predominantly Black or Mexican-American students was represented.

Test score data on the sixth-grade students and other information on their ethnic and family background, health, and attendance patterns were collected for the previous four-year period. Information on school atmosphere, management and administration, teacher characteristics, parent and teacher activities, and approaches to reading instruction were collected by interview or questionnaire. Data were analyzed to determine which factors affect reading achievement.

Findings

Armor et al. identified these factors as significantly related to reading achievement:

- Teacher training in the use of materials keyed to individual student needs
- Teachers' feelings of efficacy
- Orderly classrooms
- High levels of parent-teacher contact
- Flexibility for teachers to modify and adapt instructional approaches
- Frequent informal consultations among teachers about the reading program.

The authors found large variations in the degree of parent and community involvement among the schools studied. The key to a high degree of involvement that is well integrated into the school and its activities appears to be the leadership both of school administrators and of concerned community residents.

The following table presents a continuum of school-community interaction, from low to high.

The key to a high degree of involvement that is well integrated into the school and its activities appears to be the leadership both of school administrators and of concerned community residents.

1 School asks parents to be involved	**2** School provides projects for parents	**3** Outreach programs that benefit community, e.g. welfare or legal rights	**4** Space for parents in school provided	**5** Space with equipment or services useful to community (e.g. sewing machines)

"*In Black neighbor-hoods, the more vigorous were the schools' efforts to involve parents and community in school decision-making, the better did sixth-grade students in those schools fare in reading attain-ment.*"

Conclusions

When the predominantly African-American schools were rank-ordered by level of gains in reading achievement, then rank-ordered by level of community involvement, there was a high degree of correlation. That is, the schools with the highest gains also had the highest level of community participation. "We concluded that, in Black neighborhoods, the more vigorous were the schools' efforts to involve parents and community in school decisionmaking, the better did sixth-grade students in those schools fare in reading attainment." (p.7)

This relationship was not found, however, in the Mexican-American community, where the language barrier may have a strong interfering effect. The authors speculate that if the Hispanic community's needs and processes were better understood, a relationship between level of involvement and reading gains might be found.

See also: Cummins, Leler, Swap, Thompson.

Baker, David P. and David L. Stevenson   EJ 340 568
"Mothers' Strategies for Children's School Achievement: Managing the
Transition to High School"
Sociology of Education, Vol.59, 1986, pp.156-166

SUMMARY: In this study of 41 families with eighth-graders, the
authors explore the relationship between family socioeconomic status
(SES) and children's academic achievement, by examining actions
parents take to manage their child's school career. Although both low-
and high-SES parents are aware of useful strategies, high-SES parents
are more likely to take steps to assure their children enroll in post-
secondary education.

In the United States, children from families with high socioeconomic
status (middle-income, college-educated, and white-collar or professional) are 2.5 times more likely than low-SES children to continue
education beyond high school, and six times more likely to enter college.
This study compares actions that high- and low-SES mothers take to
manage their child's transition from eighth grade to high school, a time
when key decisions about the child's future course of study are made.

In the American educational system, unlike Europe or Japan, students
manage their educational careers in a continuous "step-by-step process,"
rather than by entering set gateways that determine their future direction. The authors suggest that "the family actively manages the child's
schooling in ways that can have substantial effects on educational
achievement." (p.157) To guide their children successfully through the
maze, parents must be aware of the school's demands, how well their
children are performing, and when and how to use their influence.

The authors interviewed 41 randomly selected mothers of eighth-
graders attending middle school in a small community of 10,000 people.
The families' SES ranged from upper-lower to upper-middle class, none
very poor or wealthy; 26 percent were non-white. The interview in-
cluded questions about the mothers' attitudes and actions on behalf of
her eighth grader's school career:
- Knowledge of and contact with school
- Knowledge of child's school performance
- Suggested and implemented homework strategies
- Suggested solutions to problems with school
- Solutions to hypothetical academic and in-school behavioral
  problems
- Specific actions taken in last year
- Family structure and socioeconomic status

From this, Baker and Stevenson developed three indicators of mother's
"schooling strategies":
1. Strategies mothers had thought of but had not necessarily used
2. Strategies mothers *did* use to gain knowledge and solve
problems
3. Child's school performance (e.g. grade point average and high
school course selection)

*"The institutional or-
ganization of
schooling in the
U.S. encompasses
a lengthy set of
specific academic
contests around
which parents
must organize their
management
strategies. Parents
must do a long
series of small
things to assist their
child toward maxi-
mum educational
attainment."*

Findings

All the mothers were involved actively in their child's school career. More than 83 percent helped their child with homework; 67 percent contacted teachers about a problem with school; 61 percent denied privileges if behavior or performance was not up to standard. The authors find "little evidence that mothers with more education know of more strategies to improve their child's school performance." (p.160) Regardless of their SES, mothers of students with high grades suggested more strategies than mothers of lower-performing students.

The next question addressed whether mothers with more education actually used more strategies and knew more about their children's life in school. In general, the higher SES mothers:

- Had more knowledge about their child's schooling--they were more likely to be able to name their child's teachers and identify their child's best and worst subjects

- Had more contact with the school--they were more likely to have met their child's teachers and to attend school events

- Steered their children toward higher education--they were more likely to select college-preparatory courses, regardless of their children's performance.

Regardless of their SES, mothers of students with high grades suggested more strategies than mothers of lower-performing students.

Although both low- and high-SES mothers are aware of strategies to improve their children's performance, high-SES mothers are more likely to use them. Low-SES mothers whose children are doing well in school also know and use these strategies, but high-SES mothers are much more likely to try to influence the school, by contacting teachers and choosing ninth-grade college-preparatory courses. Furthermore, high-SES mothers whose children are not performing well are roughly 11 times more likely to actively manage their children's critical transition to high school.

Conclusions

Whether children's options for post-secondary education remain open depends not on the socio-economic status of their family, but on how well their parents can help manage their progress through school. High-SES students tend to do better, the authors conclude, because their parents have better management skills; they are more familiar with the system, and have negotiated it successfully for themselves. "The institutional organization of schooling in the U.S. encompasses a lengthy set of specific academic contests around which parents must organize their management strategies. Parents must do a long series of small things to assist their child toward maximum educational attainment." (p.165)

See also: Lareau, Scott-Jones (1984), Stevenson and Baker, Wong Fillmore

Beane, DeAnna Banks   EJ419 429
"Say YES to a Youngster's Future (TM): A Model for Home, School and Community Partnership"
Journal of Negro Education, Vol.59, No.3, 1990, pp.360-374

SUMMARY: This article reports on the National Urban Coalition's Say YES to a Youngster's Future, which uses the Family Math and Family Science programs to develop interest in math and science among students of color. Test data on elementary school students who participated with their parents in the Say YES Saturday program in Houston show significant gains in math, reading and science, compared to non-participating students.

Reports from the National Assessment of Education Progress show that, although African-American students have more positive attitudes toward math and science than their White peers, this interest is not matched by higher achievement or greater enrollment in advanced studies of these subjects. This may be, in part, because African-American students lag far behind Whites in everyday math and science experiences, such as using a yardstick or a scale.

The Say YES program is based on the premise that students perform better when taught with activity-based math and science curricula, rather than in lecture-based classes, and when the instruction has the active support of their families and community. At the time of this report, 22 elementary schools serving low-achieving African-American and Hispanic students in three urban school districts (Houston, Washington, DC, and New Orleans) offered the program to 838 families. The program has four major objectives:

- improve the competence of math and science teachers
- increase the interests and skills of urban elementary students in math and science
- involve parents and community members in math and science education
- increase the number of students of color who are prepared for advanced levels of math and science in secondary school.

"Programs that aim to make a substantial impact on the long-term participation and performance of underrepresented children of color in mathematics and science must generate home and community support."

Key Elements of the Program

At each project site, school teams (principal, teachers, other staff) plan and implement the program. The teams also participate in summer institutes and in-service programs taught by master teachers, to develop strategies to make instruction more activity-based and to involve students' families. The teams then plan field trips and science activities for students and their families.

Once a month during the school year studied, the teams initiated Saturday morning sessions of informal math and science activities for families. Three of these were held at local zoos, museums and nature centers. Topics ranged from electricity, light, weather, and insects, to the scientific study of balls used in sports. Families used activity sheets to record, estimate, measure, classify, calculate and graph what they saw and heard. When the sessions ended, families left with simple take-home activities; thermometers, rulers and magnifying glasses were provided as needed. Often families would collaborate, helping each other or comparing observations. Back in the classroom, teachers helped students make connections between their Saturday experiences and curriculum concepts.

Findings

General assessment surveys of principals and teachers were at least 90 percent positive. Principals felt that both teachers and students were developing more interest in science and math. Teachers reported that they enjoyed teaching math and science more, and their students seemed to be learning more quickly. One teacher commented that although many parents had not finished high school and had been reluctant to help children with schoolwork, "Parents caught the fever after the first Saturday program. Now sometimes more parents than kids flock to the science learning stations." (p.370)

Data from the Metropolitan Achievement Test, given in Houston during the spring of 1987 (before the project started) and 1988, show that participating students gained in math, science and reading. The classroom performance of students whose teachers participated in the program showed significant improvement in math and reading, but not science. The grade-equivalent gains for students who participated in the Saturday program were stronger:

	Math	Science	Reading
Say YES Students	1.1	1.3	.5
Non-Participants	.7	.7	.4

This means, for example, that in math, students participating in the Saturday program gained one and one-tenth of a year for one year in school, as opposed to only seven-tenths of a year for non-participating students. Saturday students did not necessarily have participating classroom teachers; the students who made the greatest gains were those whose families were involved.

Conclusion

"While many school improvement projects can be implemented without a parent or family component, programs that aim to make a substantial impact on the long-term participation and performance of under-represented children of color in mathematics and science must generate home and community support." (p.361)

See also: Nettles, Clark (1990), Thompson.

> "Parents caught the fever after the first Saturday program. Now sometimes more parents than kids flock to the science learning stations."

Becher, Rhoda McShane   ED 247 032
"Parent involvement:
A Review of Research and Principles of Successful Practice"
National Institute of Education, Washington, DC, 1984

SUMMARY: This extensive review of the literature on parent involvement in education covers a wide range of educational research documenting the crucial role of parents in the development and education of their children, and the ways parents can be trained to improve their children's academic achievement.

In her review, the author covers four major areas:

- The role of parents and family in determining children's intelligence, competence and achievement
- The effects of parent-education programs on student achievement, and the characteristics of effective programs
- The benefits of parent involvement for schools and educators
- The principles of effective programs for parent involvement.

Findings

Examining how the effects of parent involvement influence the child, Becher found there that are several key family "process variables," or ways of behaving, that are clearly related to student achievement. Children with high achievement scores have parents who have high expectations for them, who respond to and interact with them frequently, and who see themselves as "teachers" of their children. Parents of high-scoring children also use more complex language, provide problem-solving strategies, act as models of learning and achievement, and reinforce what their children are learning in school.

Becher also found that parent-education programs, particularly those training low-income parents to work with their children, are effective in improving how well children use language skills, perform on tests, and behave in school. These programs also produce positive effects on parents' teaching styles, the way they interact with their children, and the home learning environment. The most effective programs are guided by these perspectives:

1. All parents have strengths and should know that they are valued
2. All parents can make contributions to their child's education and the school program
3. All parents have the capacity to learn developmental and educational techniques to help their children
4. All parents have perspectives on their children that can be important and useful to teachers
5. Parent-child relationships are different from teacher-child relationships

When they become involved at school, parents develop more positive attitudes about school and school personnel, help gather support in the community for the program, become more active in community affairs, develop increased self-confidence, and enroll in other educational programs.

6. Parents should be consulted in all decisions about how to involve parents
7. All parents really do care about their children.

Conclusion

There are many important effects of parent involvement on the general educational process as well as on their own child's achievement. Parents themselves develop more positive attitudes about school and school personnel, help gather support in the community for the program, become more active in community affairs, develop increased self-confidence, and enroll in other educational programs. Teachers become more proficient in their professional activities, devote more time to teaching, experiment more, and develop a more student-oriented approach. Students increase their academic achievement and cognitive development.

"In summarizing the research on parent involvement, it becomes very clear that extensive, substantial, and convincing evidence suggests that parents play a crucial role in both the home and school environments with respect to facilitating the development of intelligence, achievement, and competence in their children." (p.39)   In addition, intervention programs that encourage parents to engage in educational activities with their children are effective in improving children's cognitive development.

See Also: Gordon, Leler, Swap.

"Extensive, substantial, and convincing evidence suggests that parents play a crucial role in both the home and school environments with respect to facilitating the development of intelligence, achievement, and competence in their children."

Children with high achievement scores have parents who have high expectations for them, who respond to and interact with them frequently, and who see themselves as "teachers" of their children.

Benson, Charles S., Stuart Buckley, and Elliott A. Medrich
"Families as Educators: Time Use Contributions to School Achievement"
In School Finance Policy in the 1980's: A Decade of Conflict, Guthrie,
James, ed., Cambridge: Ballinger, 1980

SUMMARY: The authors find that elementary schoolchildren whose parents spend time with them in educational activities, or are involved in school activities, achieve more in school, regardless of socioeconomic status (SES), although different types of activities have different effects on low-income than on middle- or high-income children.

This work is part of the Children's Time Study Project at the University of California, Berkeley, using data gathered from parents of 764 sixth-graders in Oakland, California. In this study, the researchers concentrate on the relationship between specific parent-child interactions and school performance. First, types of interactions are related to SES; then within SES groups, the interactions are related to achievement. The hypothesis is that different types of activities have varying effects on achievement within each SES group.

Parent-child interactions were divided into four types:

Everyday Interactions: Eating dinner together, doing house or yard work, shopping and watching TV, going to places or events, spending weekend time together

Cultural Enrichment: Going to cultural activities, playing games together, encouraging a hobby, participating in outside programs, reading together at home

Parent Involvement: Volunteering, joining a parent-teacher organization, attending school functions

Control over Children's Activities: Rules about bedtime, chores, homework, TV, and allowances, freedom to move around outside the home, and parent pressure to follow rules.

"However, we also find that high levels of (parent) inputs are not strongly related to high achievement within the low-SES group and that on balance, parental inputs aside, their performance remains well below that of both middle- and upper-SES children."

Findings

For all SES groups taken together, "everyday interactions" and "control" show no strong relationship to achievement. "Cultural activities" and "parent involvement," however, show a significant relationship to the child's achievement. Five of the items were particularly related: visits to cultural centers, enjoying hobbies together, parent-facilitated participation in organized activities, dinnertime patterns, and doing things together on weekends.

Among low-SES children, the most effective activities were hobbies, participation in organized activities, having dinner together, and doing things on weekends. Cultural visits, although related to achievement among both high- and middle-SES children, showed no effect on low-SES children.

Conclusion

In spite of relatively severe time constraints, parents do influence their children's success in school. "In summary we do find some evidence that particular behaviors and interactions reduce the achievement deficit of low-SES children when compared with their upper SES peers." (p.34) For example, lower SES children whose parents do things with them on weekends have an achievement profile significantly different from the rest of the low SES group; in fact their achievement rates approach those of middle class children.

"However, we also find that high levels of [parent] inputs are not strongly related to high achievement within the low-SES group and that on balance, parental inputs aside, their performance remains well below that of both middle- and upper-SES children." (p.34) Low-SES children who have high parent inputs and who attend low-income schools do better than low-SES children who attend higher-income schools but have low parent inputs. In other words, parent inputs *do* reduce the proportion of low achievers, but they do not overcome the disadvantages of low-income.

See also: Baker and Stevenson, Clark (1983), Caplan et al., Dornbusch 1987, Mitrsomwang and Hawley, Snow.

"Eating dinner together is an important socializing experience, for this is perhaps the only time of day that parents and children can talk together, share and learn from one another."

Bloom, B. S.
Developing Talent in Young People
New York: Ballantine Books, 1985

SUMMARY: This study of several extremely talented young professionals who are well known in difficult, competitive fields such as
research mathematics, classical piano, other arts and sciences, and
certain sports, showed that the most common characteristic of their
general education, specialized training, and subsequent achievement
was enthusiastic parent involvement.

The author conducted far-ranging interviews with about 20-25 very
successful young people (aged 28-35) in each field, and talked extensively with their families as well. He selected the subjects for their similar
level of brilliant achievement, and then generally looked for common
features of growth and guidance that contributed to their outstanding
realization of talent.

Findings

Although the subjects varied widely in their social and ethnic background, almost all spoke of lifelong parental support for their general
education as well as for their specialized pursuits. In most cases this
support meant not only constant and direct parent involvement in
schooling, lessons, and competitions, but more important, consistent
support at home for *any* educational ambitions. Parents sent a steady
message that they completely encouraged their child's commitment to
music, science or sport.

Conclusion

In every case, the student's special training progressed beyond the
parents' expertise, rendering parent help unnecessary after an initial
phase of support; but the encouragement continued even when the
child's accomplishment excluded direct parental involvement. And in
almost every case, parent enthusiasm stood as the young star's main
confirmation that the difficult goal they were pursuing was entirely
worthwhile, and fully within their reach.

"We believe, as do the parents, that the parents' interest and participation
in the child's learning contributed significantly to his or her achievement
in the field. We find it difficult to imagine how these children could have
gotten good teachers, learned to practice regularly and thoroughly, and
developed a value of and commitment to achievement in the talent field
without a great deal of parental guidance and support." (p.476)

See also: Clark (1990), Steinberg et al.

"We find it difficult to imagine how these children could have gotten good teachers, learned to practice regularly and thoroughly, and developed a value of and commitment to achievement in the talent field without a great deal of parental guidance and support."

Bronfenbrenner, Urie   *ED 093 501*
"A Report on Longitudinal Evaluations of Preschool Programs, Vol.II: Is Early Intervention Effective?"
Office of Child Development, DHEW, 1974

SUMMARY: **This paper analyzes several studies of different educational intervention programs for disadvantaged preschool children, and discovers that those who are the subjects of early educational intervention programs show higher and more lasting gains if their mothers are actively involved in their learning.**

Bronfenbrenner contends that long-term IQ gains can be achieved by early intervention only when the parent-child relationship is properly treated, and looks at some current studies to see if they bear out his theory.

"To use a chemical analogy, parent intervention functions as a kind of fixative, which stabilizes effects produced by other processes."

Findings

Three of the studies considered by Bronfenbrenner instituted home visits by tutor/teachers, but parent involvement was voluntary and passive. They reported insignificant long-term gains.

The remaining three studies designed more active parent involvement, providing mothers with training on how to stimulate verbal interaction with their children. The most impressive, long-lasting gains were made in a 2-year program in which tutors visited homes twice a week and demonstrated toy kits to mothers and children. Less frequent sessions or training just for mothers (when children were not present) were not as effective.

"A home-based program is effective to the extent that the target is neither the child nor the parent, but the parent/child system."

Conclusion

Commenting on the "staying power" of the positive changes achieved, Bronfenbrenner says, "to use a chemical analogy, parent intervention functions as a kind of *fixative*, which stabilizes effects produced by other processes." (p.34) Although the child has no way to internalize the processes that foster growth, the parent-child system does possess that capacity. "A home-based program is effective to the extent that the target is neither the child nor the parent, but the parent/child system." (p.34)

See also: Gotts, Goodson and Hess, Guinagh and Gordon, Lazar, White et al.

Caplan, Nathan, Marcella H. Choy, and John K. Whitmore   EJ 438 367
"Indochinese Refugee Families and Academic Achievement"
Scientific American, *February 1992, pp.36-42*

SUMMARY: This study of Vietnamese, Laotian, and Chinese-Viet-namese children who emigrated to the United states in the late 1970s and early 1980s finds that their high academic success can be traced to strong family values about the importance of education, and a home environment that supports learning.

These researchers from the Institute for Social Research, University of Michigan, selected a random sample of 200 nuclear families with 536 children from a group of 1400 Southeast-Asian refugee families. This group had "limited exposure to Western culture and knew virtually no English when they arrived. Often they came with nothing more than the clothes they wore." At the time of the study they had been in the U.S. for an average of three-and-a-half years, and were attending schools in low-income metropolitan areas (Orange County, CA, Seattle, Houston, Chicago and Boston). Information was collected during interviews with parents and children in their native languages and from transcripts and related documents. In the interviews, the researchers included 26 questions about values derived from Asian literature and social science research.

The refugee children were evenly distributed among grades one through eleven, with fewer in kindergarten and 12th grade. The children's mean grade point average (GPA) was 3.05; that means most students were earning a B average. Only four percent had below a C average. Standardized test scores also showed high performance; the students' mean overall score on the California Achievement Test (CAT) was in the 54th percentile; that is, they did better than 54 percent of all those taking the test, placing just above the national average. Lowest scores were found in language and reading; the highest in math and science.

Findings

"Children often acquire a sense of their heritage as a result of deliberate and concentrated parental effort in the context of family life. This inculcation of values from one generation to another is a universal feature of the conservation of culture. We sought to determine which values were important to the parents, how well those values had been transmitted to the children, and what role values played in promoting their educational achievement." (p.39)

The researchers identified several significant values and resulting family practices that are both imbedded in the Southeastern-Asian cultural heritage and related to high achievement:

- Almost half the parents read aloud to their children, either in English or their native language; students from those families earned significantly higher grades.

Asian families contribute to their children's achievement by:

- *Reading aloud to their children*
- *Emphasizing homework on weeknights*
- *Practicing equality between the sexes in household chores*
- *Encouraging a love of learning*
- *Believing in their ability to master fate*
- *Stressing the importance of education.*

- Homework dominates weeknight activities. Parents encourage their children's studies by assuming responsibility for chores and other activities. Older children help younger ones, perhaps accounting for the higher achievement among larger families, a finding unique to Asian-Americans.

- Relative equality between the sexes, both among parents and children, was one of the strongest predictors of high GPAs. In households where fathers and boys helped with family chores, grades were significantly higher.

- "Love of learning" was rated most often by both parents and students as the factor accounting for academic success. "Both learning and imparting knowledge were perceived as pleasurable experiences rather than as drudgery."

- The families believed strongly in their potential to master their own destiny, not that luck or fate determines success.

- Other values involved an aptitude for integrating the past, present and future, which "appears to have imparted a sense of continuity and direction" to their lives.

- The families also emphasized education as the key to social acceptance and economic success.

It is interesting that two of the 26 values selected, ones to measure integration and acceptance of American ways of life, were associated with lower grades: "seeking fun and excitement" and "material possessions."

Conclusions

Earlier studies of other ethnic groups, including Jews, Japanese, and African-Americans, have also found that encouragement of academic rigor and excellence leads to high achievement. When families instill a respect for education and create a home environment that encourages learning, children do better in school.

"Yet we cannot expect the family to provide such support alone," the authors conclude. "Schools must reach out to families and engage them meaningfully in the education of their children. This involvement must go beyond annual teacher-parent meetings and must include, among other things, the identification of cultural elements that promote achievement." (p.42)

See also: Clark (1990), Mitrsomwang and Hawley, Steinberg et al., Wong Fillmore

> *"Schools must reach out to families and engage them meaningfully in the education of their children. This involvement must go beyond annual teacher-parent meetings and must include, among other things, the identification of cultural elements that promote achievement."*

Chavkin, Nancy Feyl
"School Social Workers Helping Multi-Ethnic Families, Schools,
and Communities Join Forces"
In Families and Schools in a Pluralistic Society, Chavkin, Nancy Feyl, ed.,
(Albany: State University of New York Press, 1993) Chap.12, pp.217-226

SUMMARY: This chapter describes a family, school and community collaboration in a multi-ethnic Texas district, where school social workers take the lead in identifying community services and resources for at-risk students and their families. Early evaluation results show positive gains for students.

The literature is replete with studies about why children from low-income and minority backgrounds suffer disproportionately from inadequate education and community services. The solution to this problem is more than families, schools, or community organizations can tackle alone. Only if all segments of a community join forces across ethnic and social lines, Chavkin suggests, will children get the quality of education they deserve.

In 1989, the San Marcos Consolidated Independent School District began an alternative high school for actual and potential dropouts. This center allows students to begin and complete courses at any time, and offers a self-paced curriculum that includes mentoring, counseling, tutoring, guidance and career services. Building on the success of this program, a coalition calling itself PRIDE (Positive Responsible Individuals Desiring an Education) formed between the school district and the Walter Richter Institute of Social Work at Southwest Texas State University. The district is 59 percent Hispanic, 37 percent Anglo, and four percent African-American.

The coalition has attracted several community collaborators, including the local telephone company, the chamber of commerce, the League of Latin American Citizens, and a local alcohol and drug abuse agency. Focused on the high school and pre-kindergarten levels, the program includes case management, social-worker consultation for educators and parents, a referral system to link families to social services, and a tutoring program.

In addition to keeping logs of collaborations and written accounts, or "vignettes," for each of the program approaches, PRIDE staff collect data for program planning, program monitoring, and impact assessment. At the Pre-K level, all students are screened, and those with limited English are pretested, using the Pre-Language Assessment Skills test. Then teachers complete detailed checklists of skills. At the high school level, PRIDE monitors credits earned, attendance, discipline referrals, graduation rates, and standardized test scores.

The family of a chronically absent adolescent has been transferred to safer housing and the student's attendance is nearly 100 percent.

Findings

The most impressive results are found in the vignettes, which report dramatic turn-arounds for students with chronic academic and social adjustment problems. Parents in remote areas receive help in using home-learning activities; a student with a cocaine addiction is attending a community drug rehabilitation program as an outpatient and is also back in class; a seventeen-year-old who refused to speak in public is now attending counseling with her elderly widowed father and is working to become a tutor for pre-K students; the family of a chronically absent adolescent has been transferred to safer housing and the student's attendance is nearly 100 percent.

For the pre-K program, data show at least a one-stage gain for limited-English students in their first year; all students increase their preschool readiness scores. At the high school level, the district-wide drop-out rate has decreased from eight to six percent.

Conclusion

"As the Coalition for PRIDE illustrates, the interrelationships among small units of a social system are of primary importance. Family, school, and community are key elements in the educational process, and all three parts of the system must work together for the educational process to be successful." (p.224)

See also: Clark (1990), Comer, Kellaghan et al., Swap.

"Family, school, and community are key elements in the educational process, and all three parts of the system must work together for the educational process to be successful."

Clark, Reginald M.
Family Life and School Achievement: Why Poor Black Children Succeed
or Fail
Chicago: University of Chicago Press, 1983

**SUMMARY: An intensely focused study of ten poor, Black families
and their high school children finds that a family's overall cultural
style, not marital status, educational level, income, or social surround-
ings, is what determines whether children are prepared for competent
performance at school.**

Some poor Black families produce children who do well in school; others
do not. Convinced that family characteristics traditionally used in
educational research, such as income level, mother's educational background, parents' marital status, ethnicity, and so on, do not explain why
children succeed or fall behind, Clark conducted in-depth case studies
of ten families living in Chicago public housing projects. Five families
included senior high school students performing academically in the top
20 percent of their class; five included senior high school students in the
bottom 20 percent of their class.

To demonstrate that the number of parents at home is not necessarily
related to achievement, Clark selected both one and two-parent families
for each category:

Family Type	Successful Students	Less Successful Students
One Parent	3	2
Two Parents	2	3

Clark visited with each family for at least two days and observed its
structure and interrelationships within the following framework:

1. **Family theme and background:** Names and nicknames, ages,
religion, residence, educational backgrounds, social history, group
affiliations

2. **Early child-rearing and family practices:** Events of child's for-
mative years, early training and value orientation, early family
dynamics

3. **Mental health:** Student's values, attitudes, and personality

4. **Home living patterns:** Routine patterns such as living arrangements and money handling, family relations, rules of the house,
power relationships, methods of discipline, parents' approach to
student's time and space, division of labor

5. **Intellectuality at home:** Approach to homework, study, and other
educational activities, aspirations and expectations of parents and

*"Families whose
members are emo-
tionally able to
love, cooperate,
support one
another, and find
some support out-
side the home are
usually more
satisfied with their
lives." (p.210)*

*"The wonder is not
that so many are
ruined but that so
many survive."
--James Baldwin*

High achieving families were characterized by
- *frequent dialogues between parents and children,*
- *strong parent encouragement of academic pursuits,*
- *clear and consistent limits for children,*
- *warm and nurturing interactions,*
- *consistent monitoring of how time is used.*

children, contact with the school, parents' monitoring and instructional activities.

Findings

Clark found that in the high-achievers' homes, regardless of whether the family had one or two parents, certain patterns appeared time and again. These families were characterized by frequent dialogues between parents and children, strong parent encouragement of academic pursuits, clear and consistent limits for children, warm and nurturing interactions, and consistent monitoring of how time is used. Clark terms this style of parenting "sponsored independence" and points out that it is also known as "authoritative."

Parents of high-achieving children also seem to hold common attitudes toward education. They are willing to put their children's growth and development before their own, and they feel responsible for helping their children gain a general fund of knowledge and basic literacy skills. These parents also feel that pursuing knowledge is their *children's* responsibility and expect them to participate in some form of postsecondary school training.

In terms of their relationship to the school, parents of children who do well show great concern about the school's success with its students and believe that only with parent input will the school provide sound training. These parents also visit the school periodically, get acquainted with the teachers, and become involved in various activities.

About the parents of less successful children, Clark describes the circumstances of their lives and quotes James Baldwin, "...the wonder is not that so many are ruined but that so many survive." Their parenting style is one Clark terms "unsponsored independence" and is marked by loose social ties and less parent vigilance in supervision. The students recalled few instances when teachers provided encouragement for their efforts, and their classroom experiences had fostered negative expectations of success. Parents almost never visited the school, except in response to a negative report, and certainly never paid a spontaneous call on their children's teachers. There was no positive, reinforcing pattern of school-home encouragement.

Conclusion

Clark concludes that "...it is the overall *quality* of the family's life-style, not the composition, or status, or some subset of family process dynamics, that determines whether children are prepared for academically competent performance in the classroom." (p.1)

See also: Benson et al., Milne, Rumberger, Dornbusch, Ziegler.

Clark, Reginald M.
"Why Disadvantaged Students Succeed: What Happens Outside School Is Critical"
Public Welfare, *Spring 1990, pp.17-23*

SUMMARY: In this report on his research with Black 12th-graders in Chicago and with Hispanic, Asian, African-American, and Anglo elementary, middle and high school students in Los Angeles, Clark finds that high-achieving students typically spend approximately 20 hours a week engaged in "constructive learning activity" after school.

Although the term "disadvantaged" is often associated with particular circumstances, such as low income or unhealthy living environments, Clark points out that, ultimately, educational disadvantage might be defined as the lack of necessary conditions for educational and occupational success. Many youngsters with apparently "disadvantaged" backgrounds perform well in school and in later life because their social circumstances have been mediated by behaviors and attitudes that allow them to achieve.

If learning can be understood as the result of interpersonal communications in everyday life, Clark argues, then the difference between high- and low-achieving youngsters from similar backgrounds might be explained by how and with whom they spend their time -- particularly the 70 percent of their waking hours that are outside of school.

"The attitudes and relationships between youngsters and their parents, relatives, teachers, ministers, coaches, instructors, and tutors can be among the most important factors in creating an environment that will maximize the chances for success--during their school years and throughout their lives."

Findings

High-achieving children from all backgrounds tend to spend approximately 20 hours a week in constructive learning activities outside of school. Supportive guidance from adults is a critical factor in whether such opportunities are available.

"In a given week, this would consist of four or five hours of discussion with knowledgeable adults or peers; four or five hours of leisure reading; one or two hours of various types of writing, such as grocery lists, telephone messages, letters, or diary entries; five or six hours of homework or study; several hours devoted to hobbies; two or three hours of chores; and four to five hours of games." (p.19)

Five categories of activity provide young people opportunities to engage in stimulating mental workouts:

- Professionally guided, formal learning activities
- Deliberate out-of-school learning and work activities (homework, lessons, practice, volunteer work)
- High-yield leisure activities (reading, writing, conversation, problem-solving, visiting museums)
- Recreational activities (sports, movies, biking, talking on the telephone)

- Health maintenance activities (exercising, going to church, grooming, meditating).

The first type is most often provided in school, but the amount of time actually engaged in learning may vary from 7.5 hours a week in poorly organized classrooms to 17.5 hours in the best settings. The remaining activities occur outside the school day, although schools may sponsor some of them, such as sports, clubs, and tutoring.

Whether these activities are "high yield," in terms of their potential for learning and development, depends on four "quality indicators":

1. Time spent on a particular learning task

2. Opportunity to become actively involved in thinking while doing the task

3. Extent of supportive input by knowledgeable adults and peers

4. Standards, expectations and goals that surround the activity.

Conclusion

Providing these constructive activities is the responsibility not just of the family, but of adults in the school and community as well. In fact, adult modeling is crucial. "The attitudes and relationships between youngsters and their parents, relatives, teachers, ministers, coaches, instructors, and tutors can be among the most important factors in creating an environment that will maximize the chances for success-- during their school years and throughout their lives." (p.23)

See also: Benson et al, Caplan et al., Clark (1983, 1993), Mitrsomwang and Hawley.

High-achieving students typically spend approximately 20 hours a week engaged in "constructive learning activity" after school.

The difference between high- and low-achieving youngsters from similar back- grounds might be explained by how and with whom they spend their time -- particularly the 70 percent of their waking hours that are outside of school.

Clark, Reginald M.
"Homework-Focused Parenting Practices That Positively Affect Student Achievement"
In Families and Schools in a Pluralistic Society, *Chavkin, Nancy Feyl, ed., (Albany: State University of New York Press, 1993) Chap.4, pp.85-105*

SUMMARY: This study of low- and high-achieving third-graders in Los Angeles finds that high achievers tend to come from families in which parents set high standards for their children's educational activities and maintain a home environment that supports learning.

In recent years, researchers have shifted their focus from family background factors such as income and educational level, which were thought to determine achievement levels, to family attitudes and behaviors that can promote high achievement among students from all backgrounds. This study was designed to explore whether certain parenting practices related to homework and studying can promote high achievement, and whether those practices are associated with parents' education, family structure, and ethnic background.

Clark drew a sample of 1,141 third-grade students from 71 Los Angeles elementary schools that have computerized student records. The sample was divided into two groups, high achievers (scoring at or above the 50th percentile on the Comprehensive Test of Basic Skills) and low achievers (scoring at or below the 25th percentile). The students were predominantly Hispanic, Black, Asian, or other non-Anglo. Data were gathered through a questionnaire sent to the parents of the sample students, to learn about parents' perceptions of and practices toward homework, how their children handle homework assignments, and family background. The response rate was 40 percent; 304 questionnaires were returned from parents of low achievers, 156 from parents of high achievers.

The parents of high achievers were more involved in home learning activities, their children spent more time on homework, and they used the dictionary more.

Findings

Most parents talk to their children about homework, read to their children, and make sure they do their assignments. On many of the variables Clark measured, there was no significant difference between parents of high achievers and low achievers. However, the parents of high achievers were more involved in home learning activities, their children spent more time on homework, and they used the dictionary more. On the other hand, parents of low achievers assisted their children with homework more and spoke English at home more often.

In terms of family background, low achievers tended to come from homes where the parents were younger, were not employed outside the home, had not been to college, were low-income and receiving public assistance, and had more than two children. Even though the higher-achieving students often had parents who were not home to monitor their children's activities between 3 and 5 PM, their participation in the work force was related to higher test scores.

Two clusters of variables, parent's press for the child's academic success, and family circumstances and resources for achievement, were significantly related to higher achievement:

High achievers came from a wide variety of family backgrounds. "Let us recall that 51.3 percent of the mothers of high achievers possessed no more than a high school education."

Factor	Variable	% Variance
Parent's press for child's academic success	**Parent perception of frequency of homework**	**47.2**
	Parent perception of child's homework engagement	
	Child knows how to use dictionary	
	Parent expectation for child's education	
Family circumstances and resources for achievement	**Parent knowledge of how to help**	**41.7**
	Mother's unemployment status	
	Number of children living at home	

"To be academically successful, students apparently needed their parents (or other adults) to expose them to an array of additional support behaviors."

Despite the relationship between achievement and family resources, Clark found that high achievers came from a wide variety of family backgrounds. "Let us recall that 51.3 percent of the mothers of high achievers possessed no more than a high school education. Almost 40 percent...lived in single parent households. Almost 43 percent of the high achievers were Hispanic and 21.8 percent were Black." (p.103)

Conclusion

"Results of these analyses revealed that home process variables, parental personality variables, and family background circumstances worked together to shape student achievement patterns. The data showed that most parents of both high- and low-achieving students were enacting some of the positive behaviors that contribute to student achievement....However, to be academically successful, students apparently needed their parents (or other adults) to expose them to an array of additional support behaviors." (p.103)

See also: Epstein, Snow, et al. Stevenson and Baker, Walberg.

Cochran, Moncrieff, and Henderson, Charles R., Jr.   ED 262 862
"Family Matters: Evaluation of the Parental Empowerment Program"
Cornell University, Ithaca, NY, 1986

SUMMARY: An intensive, family-oriented, early-childhood intervention program featuring home visits and neighborhood-based parent support groups produced positive effects in student achievement when the children entered public school, especially for children from two-parent families and from low-income families.

The program was offered to 160 families, each with a three-year-old child, in ten different neighborhoods in Syracuse, New York. Paraprofessionals were trained to give information about child rearing and to demonstrate examples of parent-child learning activities in a series of home visits designed to reinforce the parents' feelings of importance and effectiveness.

Once the workers and families were introduced, group meetings among neighboring project families were arranged. At the meetings, families were encouraged to turn to one another as resources. Families participated for twenty-four months, until the children entered school; then follow-up data on student performance were collected, based on report cards and teacher evaluation.

Findings

The findings were subjected to in-depth analysis based on family structure (married/unmarried), income, race (Black/White), education (more or less than 12 years), parent perceptions of effectiveness, parent-child activities, types of communication with the school, and development of a family support network. All were compared to a matched control group. Although the results varied according to race, income, and family structure, involvement in the program for all categories of families resulted in better performance of their children in school. On the average, low-income children in the program performed as well as children with middle-class, married parents who were not in the program.

It is not possible to describe all the variations of program effects here, but the researchers did note that children of single parents tended to do less well in school, unless parents were able to develop a social support network. This strongly suggests that couples are better able to use their experiences to help their children develop, while single parents need to develop self-confidence and a network of support before they can benefit. "Parents with positive and realistic views of their capacities as parents are likely to make good use of available social supports and place high priority on activities with their children."(p.68) This, in turn, leads to their children's success in school.

On the average, low-income children in the program performed as well as children with middle-class, married parents who were not in the program.

"Parents with positive and realistic views of their capacities as parents are likely to make good use of available social supports and place high priority on activities with their children."

> "Empowerment will
> only result...from
> acknowledging
> and making clear
> to parents that
> they are valuable
> allies in the educa-
> tional process, with
> a great deal to
> offer."

Conclusions

The authors conclude that the school can be a powerful force for building parent capacity and thereby buffer the negative consequences of low income--without major alteration of its basic educational mission.

First, school personnel can strengthen parents' appreciation of their important role by providing positive feedback at every opportunity. Communications between home and school should be positive and preventive rather than negative and remedial. Second, schools can strengthen informal social supports for parents, by such simple means as providing a list of children's names, addresses and phone numbers, holding get-togethers, and sponsoring a parent organization. Third, staff can provide parents with information and materials to help them work with their children at home, to complement and reinforce what is being taught at school.

"Empowerment will only result...from acknowledging and making clear to parents that they are valuable allies in the educational process, with a great deal to offer." (p.68)

See also: Cummins, Gordon, Sattes, Schweinhart and Weikart.

Coleman, James S. and Thomas Hoffer
Public and Private High Schools: The Impact of Communities
New York: Basic Books, Inc., 1987

SUMMARY: In this continuation of their 1982 study, the authors find that students in private and Catholic high schools perform better than students from comparable backgrounds in public schools, and they speculate that the critical difference lies in the relationship of schools to the communities they serve.

In 1980, the National Center for Education Statistics, an arm of the U.S. Department of Education, sponsored the High School and Beyond Survey, a large-scale study of sophomores and seniors in 1015 public and private high schools. Coleman and Hoffer were asked to look at the data collected to examine two questions related to private schools: the extent to which private schools affect racial/religious/income divisions in society, and the relative academic performance of private vs. public schools.

Findings

The resulting study, *High School Achievement* (1982), found that students in private and Catholic schools performed approximately one grade level higher on standardized tests of verbal and math achievement than their comparable public school counterparts. In Catholic schools, this effectiveness was especially pronounced for students from "disadvantaged backgrounds," that is, those with less-well-educated parents and from Black and Hispanic families. The authors also found that private schools do not contribute measurably to racial or economic segregation.

In 1982, the National Center for Education Statistics (NCES) collected follow-up data on the students who were seniors in 1980. This made it possible for the authors to double-check their conclusions and to do additional analysis. According to that data, not only do students who attend private and Catholic schools do better in school, they are also more likely to graduate, to enroll in college, and to continue their college studies once enrolled.

The authors speculate that the reason for the difference in student performance lies in the relationship between families and the schools. Public schools, they contend, see themselves as an instrument of society intended to free the child from constraints imposed by the accident of birth. Private schools, on the other hand, see the school as an agent of the family, as an extension of the parents' will. Catholic schools act as an agent of the religious community of which the family is a part; private schools are agents of the parents in a more individualistic sense.

One indication of the difference in relationships between schools and families is the level of parent involvement. The following chart,

"The social capital that exists in the community, its power to make and enforce norms for the youth of the school, is not fixed and immutable but can be affected by the actions of the school."

reproduced from the book, indicates that the percentage of private- and Catholic-school parents who are involved in their children's education is higher than that in public schools:

Annual parent activities	Public	Catholic	Private	Elite Private
Parent-Teacher Conference	39.2%	56.4%	47.3%	64.4%
PTA Meeting	19.9	35.1	33.3	23.8
Visiting Classes	21.0	25.2	22.9	26.8
Contacting Educator if Student Had Problem	45.5	43.1	49.8	51.6
Volunteer Work	27.2	45.8	43.6	47.2

> "One of the most important factors in a child's success in school is the degree to which his or her parents are actively involved in the child's education."

These figures on parent participation in school affairs reveal that parent involvement is significantly lower in public than in Catholic schools. In public schools, the highest level of parent-school interaction occurs if the student has a problem. For Catholic schools, these disparities do not appear to be explained by difference in family backgrounds, although for other private school parents, income and educational advantages do seem to explain the disparity. The authors feel this underscores their argument that the functional community around the Catholic school induces parents who would otherwise be uninvolved to participate.

The authors devote considerable analysis to their thesis that the Catholic-school community works to overcome disadvantages such as low income and educational levels, and single or working parents. They also find within Catholic schools a greater achievement effect for Catholic students than non-Catholic, and for Catholic students who are attend church. The same effect appears on drop-out rates.

Conclusions

What are the implications for public schools? The authors recommend increasing the social resources available to students through organizing collective events, giving students more intensive contact with a smaller number of teachers, and strengthening the relations of parents with one another and with the school. "(O)ne of the most important factors in a child's success in school is the degree to which his or her parents are actively involved in the child's education." (p.52)

Educators must recognize "that the social capital that exists in the community, its power to make and enforce norms for the youth of the school, is not fixed and immutable but can be affected by the actions of the school."

See also: Cummins, Melnick and Fiene, McDill, Wong Fillmore.

Comer, James P.
"Educating Poor Minority Children"
Scientific American, Vol.259, No.5, November 1988, pp.2-8

SUMMARY: This article describes a long-term program to transform two chronically low-achieving, inner-city New Haven elementary schools, partly by including massive parent involvement, which achieved dramatic, lasting gains in student academic success.

Deeply concerned about the chronic low achievement of poor, minority children, Comer began in the 1960s to speculate that the contrast between these children's experiences at home and those at school deeply affects their psychological development. "The failure to bridge the social and cultural gap between home and school may lie at the root of the poor academic performance of many of these children," the author asserts. (p.3)

In 1968, Comer and his colleagues at the Yale Child Study Center initiated a long-term collaboration with the two New Haven schools whose populations were 99 percent Black and almost entirely low-income. Both ranked near the bottom in achievement and attendance among the 33 schools in the city, and there were serious problems with attendance and discipline, as well as high staff turnover.

The program Comer developed was guided by an important principle: children learn from people they bond to. In Comer's words:

"A child from a poor, marginal family (in contrast to middle-class children) is likely to enter school without adequate preparation. The child may arrive without ever having learned such social skills as negotiation and compromise. A child who is expected to read at school may come from a home where no one reads and may never have heard a parent read bedtime stories. The child's language skills may be underdeveloped or non-standard. Expectations at home and at school may be radically at odds. For example, in some families a child who does not fight back will be punished. And yet the same behavior will get the child into trouble at school." (p.5)

The consequences of this alienation become apparent by the time children are eight, or in third grade, when the curriculum begins to require them to progress more rapidly than their level of development may allow. At this age, children begin to understand how they and their families are different in income, culture and style from the people who work at the school, making the necessary bond extremely difficult to nurture.

If the key to raising academic achievement is to promote psychological development, thereby encouraging bonding to the school, the school must promote positive interaction between parents and staff. To develop this relationship, each school in Comer's program created a governance and management team led by the principal and made up of elected parents and teachers, as well as a mental-health specialist and a member

The program Comer developed was guided by an important principle: children learn from people they bond to.

If the key to raising academic achievement is to promote psychological development, thereby encouraging bonding to the school, the school must promote positive interaction between parents and staff.

"Typical schools, with their hierarchical and authoritarian structure, cannot give underdeveloped or differently developed students the skills and experiences that will enable them to fulfill expectations at the school. Instead, such students are labeled "bad," unmotivated or stupid." (p.6)

"Policy-makers must recognize that students' social development is as important to society as their academic ability."

of the support staff. The teams decided issues relating to the school's academic and social programs as well as school procedures. Three rules guided the team:

1. Team members had to recognize the authority of the principal, but the principal had to weigh the others' concerns before making a decision

2. Efforts were to focus on problem-solving, not on placing blame

3. Decisions were made by consensus, not by vote.

Because so many students had emotional, learning, and behavioral problems, the team created a mental health group to handle each case and to recommend changes in school policies and practices that impeded student development. Many programs emerged in response to the students' needs. In one school, children stayed with one teacher for two years. A Discovery Room allowed "turned off" children to form a trusting relationship with an adult, and rekindle an interest in learning, through play. Staff and parents devised a curriculum of social skills, through which children learned how to write invitations, serve as hosts, and plan social activities.

Results

During the first five years, both schools attained the best attendance records in the city and near-grade-level performance; at the same time, student behavior problems were reduced significantly. By 1979, and without any change in the socioeconomic makeup of the schools, students in the fourth grade were performing at grade level. By 1984, fourth-graders in the two schools ranked third and fourth highest on the Iowa Test of Basic Skills. Comer notes that there have been no serious behavior problems at either school in more than a decade.

Conclusion

"All the money and effort expended for educational reform will have only limited benefits--particularly for poor, minority children--as long as the underlying developmental and social issues remain unaddressed....[Policy-makers] must recognize that students' social development is as important to society as their academic ability." (p.8)

See also: Comer and Haynes, Cummins, Swap, Wong Fillmore.

Comer, James P., and Norris M. Haynes
"Summary of School Development Program Effects"
New Haven, CT: Yale Child Study Center, June 1992

SUMMARY: This paper summarizes evaluation findings on the School Development Program (SDP) developed by Dr. Comer. At three sites, Benton Harbor, MI, Prince George's County, MD, and New Haven, CT, researchers found that, compared to control groups, students in the predominantly low-income SDP elementary and middle schools improved in four areas: academic performance in reading and math, behavior and adjustment to school, self-concept, and positive ratings of classroom climate.

The School Development Program, developed in New Haven by Dr. Comer and his colleagues at the Yale Child Study Center, has several guiding principles:

> 1. A no-fault approach, focusing not on who is to blame, but on what can be done
> 2. Coordination and cooperation among all adults concerned with the child's best educational interests
> 3. Decision by consensus whenever possible
> 4. Regular meetings representing the entire school community
> 5. Active involvement of parents every step of the way.

The vehicle for improvement is the School Governance and Management Team, representing the school principal and the school community: teachers, parents, instructional aides, counselors, custodians, and support staff. This group designs a comprehensive school plan that addresses the social climate, academic climate and goals, staff development, and assessment. Subcommittees address specific areas of the plan, such as attendance, community and parent relations, and instructional strategies.

SDP schools typically have frequent social events for staff and families, parent education classes, volunteer programs, and extensive parent involvement on the subcommittees and throughout the school building. The studies covered in this report were not designed to reveal whether some SDP components had greater effects on achievement than others.

Academic Effects

- A 1986 analysis of elementary-grade achievement data in Benton Harbor showed significant four-year average gains for SDP students in reading and math. Students in SDP schools gained between 7.5 and 11 percentile points, exceeding gains for the district as a whole.
- A 1987 study in Prince George's County showed that SDP third- and fifth-grade students experienced nearly twice the level of gain in California Achievement Test reading and math scores as

A 1987 study in Prince George's County showed that SDP third- and fifth-grade students showed nearly twice the level of gain in California Achievement Test reading and math scores as did the district as a whole.

did the district as a whole. These gains were further linked to the degree and quality of SDP implementation.

- A trend analysis of SDP fourth-graders in New Haven showed steady gains between 1969 and 1984. Their grade equivalent scores increased from about 3.0 in reading and math to 6.0 in reading and 5.0 in math over the fifteen-year period.

- Several studies comparing SDP schools with matched control schools reported significant differences in achievement. A 1987 study of seventh-graders showed higher math scores and grade point averages among SDP students. A 1988 study showed positive changes over one year among SDP elementary school students in reading, math and language on the California Achievement Test. A 1988 retrospective study found significant differences for SDP sixth-graders (but not eighth-graders) in math and language on the Metropolitan Achievement Test.

Behavior and School Adjustment Effects

- Data from 1982 to 1985 in Benton Harbor show significantly greater declines in student suspensions, absences, and corporal punishment rates in SDP schools compared to the district as a whole. "For example, SDP schools recorded a 19 percent decline in suspension days, compared to a 35 percent *increase*...for the district as a whole." (emphasis added, p.4)

- Experimental control studies conducted in 1988 and 1989 across the four districts indicate that "SDP students experienced significantly greater positive changes in attendance, and teacher ratings of classroom behavior, attitude toward authority, and group participation when compared to non-SDP students." (p.4)

Self-Concept

According to a 1990 study, SDP students in the fourth and sixth grades across sites scored significantly higher than the control group on six self-concept dimensions, and higher than the national normative group on total self-concept, as measured by the Piers Harris Self-Concept scale.

Classroom and School Climate

In a 1988 study of 288 students, students in SDP schools gave significantly more positive assessments of their classroom climate than non-SDP students, using the Classroom Environment Scale. In addition, parents and teachers in SDP schools also rated school climate significantly higher than their non-SDP counterparts.

Conclusion

Comer and Haynes conclude that "efforts to document the effects of SDP have been consistent with our philosophy that educational improvement embodies academic as well as personal and social growth." (p.1)

See also: Comer, Cummins, Swap, Thompson.

"SDP students experienced significantly greater positive changes in attendance, and teacher ratings of classroom behavior, attitude toward authority, and group participation when compared to non-SDP students."

Cummins, Jim   *EJ 330 827*
"Empowering Minority Students: A Framework for Intervention"
Harvard Educational Review, *Vol.56, No.1, February 1986*

SUMMARY: Citing programs that have been successful in promoting achievement of minority group students, the author proposes a theoretical framework for changing the relationship between educators and students that includes substantial family and community participation.

Despite costly attempts to reverse low achievement among minority group students in the United States, their drop-out rates and over-representation in special programs remain unacceptably high. These reform attempts have not been successful, Cummins argues, because the relationships between teachers and students have remained unchanged.

As a preface, Cummins discusses the debate over bilingual education programs. Those who favor bilingual instruction argue that children should be taught in a language they understand; those who favor English immersion argue that children learning in Spanish will not succeed in an English-speaking environment. Both arguments, he says, are inadequate to explain the underlying reasons why students learn--or reject--the dominant language. Extensive studies show that if "instruction through a minority language is effective in developing academic proficiency in the minority language, transfer of this proficiency to the majority language will occur given adequate exposure and motivation to learn the majority language."

The Framework

The central principle of the framework is that students from "dominated" minority groups can be either "empowered" or "disabled" by their interactions with educators. Citing research on international patterns of minority group failure by John Ogbu and others, Cummins concludes that "power and status relations between minority and majority groups exert a major influence on school performance." Minority groups of low status (Burakumin in Japan, Finns in Sweden, Blacks in the U.S.) internalize their inferior status and fail to perform well in school.

On the other hand, school failure does not occur in minority groups that (1) remain positively oriented toward both their own and the dominant culture, (2) do not perceive themselves as inferior to the dominant group, and (3) are not alienated from their own cultural values (e.g. Asian-Americans, Jews).

If members of minority groups are disabled by their interactions with the dominant society's institutions, minority students can still succeed in education to the extent that the patterns of interaction in school reverse those that prevail in society.

Students from "dominated" minority groups can be either "empowered" or "disabled" by their interactions with educators.

Schools that empower their minority students have four major characteristics:

> 1.**Additive**: The students' language and culture are incorporated into the school program
> 2.**Collaborative**: Family and community participation is encouraged as an integral component of children's education
> 3.**Interaction-Oriented**: Children are motivated to use language actively in gaining knowledge for their own use
> 4.**Advocacy-Oriented**: Educators become advocates for the students rather than labeling students as having a "problem."

Findings

The Spanish-only preschool program of the Carpinteria school district in California has incorporated these principles, in response to data showing that most Spanish-speaking children entering kindergarten lacked the skills needed to succeed. In addition to developing the children's language skills in Spanish, the program encourages parents to be their children's first teachers and to provide language experiences for them at home.

Not only did the program graduates score nearly as high as English-speaking students on the School Readiness Inventory, but their scores were significantly higher than Spanish-speaking children who graduated from a traditional, English-only program. At the entrance to first grade, 47 percent of the experimental program students were fluent in English, compared to 10 percent of other Spanish-background students.

Program evaluators also found that the parent-involvement component made a significant difference. "The parents of project participants are much more aware of and involved in their children's school experience than non-participant parents of Spanish-speakers. This is seen as having a positive impact on the future success of the project participants--the greater the involvement of parents, the greater the chances of success of the child."

Conclusion

If programs that respect the students' cultural identity and language can result in significantly higher achievement, it can also be true that programs treating their background as deficient can disable them. In a preschool program where their cultural identity was reinforced, where there was active collaboration with parents, and where meaningful use of language was part of all daily activities, students developed high levels of conceptual and linguistic skills in *both* English and Spanish.

See also: Comer (1988), Gordon, Swap, Wong Fillmore.

In a preschool program where:
- *cultural identity was reinforced,*
- *there was active collaboration with parents,*
- *meaningful use of language was part of all daily activities,*

students developed high levels of conceptual and linguistic skills in both English and Spanish.

Dauber, Susan and Joyce Epstein
"Parent Attitudes and Practices of Involvement in Inner-City Elementary and
Middle Schools"
In Families and Schools in a Pluralistic Society, *Chavkin, Nancy Feyl, ed.,*
(Albany: State University of New York Press, 1993), Chap.2, pp.53-71

**SUMMARY: This report on a survey of 2,317 inner-city elementary-
and middle-school parents finds that the level of parent involvement
is directly linked to the specific practices that schools and teachers use
to encourage involvement at school and to guide parents in how to
help their children at home. The authors also assert that parents who
are more involved tend to have children who are performing better in
school.**

Building on their earlier work with teachers in inner-city Baltimore
schools (see Epstein, 1991), the researchers asked parents about their
attitudes about their children's schools, their practices at home, their
perceptions of how the schools currently involve parents, and their
preferences for actions and programs by the schools. Five elementary
and three middle schools serving low-income neighborhoods were
selected at random from sets of similar schools. More than 50 percent of
the parents in each school responded to the questionnaire developed by
the authors, in collaboration with teacher representatives from each
school.

The main gauges used to measure parents' practices were:
- Parent involvement at the school--frequency of helping at the
  school building
- Parent involvement with homework--frequency of assisting and
  monitoring homework
- Parent involvement in reading activities at home--frequency of
  parents' helping students with reading
- Total parent involvement--frequency of parents' use of all types
  of involvement, including games, chores and trips.

Parents also rated their children's schools on nine parent-involvement
practices, from informing parents about how the child is doing in school,
to guiding them in ways to help the child at home. Other measures
included parent attitudes about the school, family background, and
parent ratings of their children's performance in school.

*"The strongest and
most consistent
predictors of
parent involve-
ment at school
and at home are
the specific school
programs and
teacher practices
that encourage
and guide parent
involvement."*

Findings

Parents of elementary schoolchildren are more involved than parents
with children in the middle grades, in large part because elementary
school teachers do more to involve parents in the school and at home.
In all cases, parents with more education are more involved both at home
and school. Parents were also more involved if their children were better
students, although this does not necessarily mean that the children do
better because the parents are involved. The authors suggest that
"parents whose children are doing well or are doing better in school are

more likely to do more to ensure their children's continued success." (p.60)

"The strongest and most consistent predictors of parent involvement at school and at home are the specific school programs and teacher practices that encourage and guide parent involvement." (p.61) Regardless of family background or student grade level, parents are more likely to become partners in their children's education if they feel that the schools have strong practices to involve parents with homework and reading activities both at school and at home.

Conclusions

Most parents believe their children attend a good school and that the teachers care about their children. This attitude is directly related to the extent to which teachers work to involve parents; the more the school works with parents, the more highly the parents rate the school. Parents want teachers to advise them how to help their children at home, and they want more information about the curriculum. Inner-city parents also want information and assistance to help develop the special qualities and talents they see in their children.

Although the teachers in these urban schools report that most parents are not involved, and don't want to be, the parents tell a different story. Not only are they involved in helping their children learn, they want more and better information from teachers about how to help. "The implication is that all schools, including inner-city schools, can develop more comprehensive programs of parent involvement to help more families become knowledgeable partners in their children's education." (p.69)

See also: Epstein, Leler, Tizard et al.

"All schools, including inner-city schools, can develop more comprehensive programs of parent involvement to help more families become knowledgeable partners in their children's education."

Dornbusch, Sanford, Phillip Ritter, P. Herbert Leiderman, Donald F.
Roberts, and Michael Fraleigh   EJ362 728
"The Relation of Parenting Style to Adolescent School Performance"
Child Development, Vol.58., No.5, October 1987, pp.1244-1257

SUMMARY: A study of San Francisco-area high school students documents significant and very consistent relationships between parenting styles and student grades.

To study the relative effects of different parenting styles on student
performance, the authors distributed a questionnaire to 7,836 students
attending six high schools in the San Francisco Bay Area. About 88
percent of the total enrollment responded. Additional data were
gathered from an earlier survey (1983) of students in five of the same
schools, and from a family questionnaire sent to the homes of all students
in the later sample. Questions covered student background, self-
reported grades, perceptions of parent attitudes and behavior, and
family communication patterns.

Three parenting styles are identified and correlated with student grades,
parent education levels, ethnicity, and family structure:

- **Authoritarian:** Parents tell children not to argue with or question
  adults, punish children for poor grades, and respond to good
  grades with instructions to do even better.

- **Permissive:** Parents seem indifferent to grades, whether poor or
  good, do not stress working hard, establish no rules about watching television, and are not involved in education, either at home
  or at school.

- **Authoritative:** Parents tell children to look at both sides of an
  issue and admit that kids sometimes know more; they talk about
  family politics and encourage all family members to participate
  in decisions; they respond to good grades with praise, to bad
  grades with some restrictions and offers of help and encouragement.

Findings

Across ethnic groups, education levels, and family structures, the
authors consistently found that authoritarian parenting was associated
with the lowest grades, permissive parenting with the next lowest, and
authoritative with the highest grades. Inconsistent parenting, or switch-
ing from one style to the other, is strongly associated with low grades.

There are, however, some interesting subcategories of
response. Hispanic females react very negatively to authoritarian
parenting, but Hispanic males do not. Asian students do well in school
regardless of parenting styles, although there is a negative relationship

*Across ethnic
groups, education
levels, and family
structures,
authoritarian
parenting was as-
sociated with the
lowest grades, per-
missive parenting
with the next
lowest, and
authoritative with
the highest
grades.*

*Parenting style, or
variations in family
processes, is a
more powerful
predictor of stu-
dent achievement
than parent
education, eth-
nicity, or family
structure.*

In "authoritative" families, parents:

- *tell children to look at both sides of an issue and admit that kids sometimes know more*
- *talk about family politics and encourage all family members to participate in decisions*
- *respond to good grades with praise*
- *react to bad grades with some restrictions and offers of help and encouragement.*

with authoritarian parenting. Students from single-parent families tend to do less well; their parents' styles tend to be permissive or inconsistent.

Conclusion

Parenting style, or variations in family processes, is a more powerful predictor of student achievement than parent education, ethnicity, or family structure. Students whose parents are authoritative do better than similar students whose parents are permissive or authoritarian.

See also: Clark (1983, 1990), Kellaghan, Steinberg et al., Ziegler.

Eagle, Eva   ED 307 332
"Socioeconomic Status, Family Structure, and Parental Involvement: The
Correlates of Achievement"
Paper presented at the Annual Meeting of the American Educational Research
Association, San Francisco, March 27-31, 1989

SUMMARY: This study assesses the varying effects of socioeconomic status (SES), parent attention, mother's working patterns, and family structure on high school student achievement. Although parent education level and income are associated with higher achievement, when SES is controlled, only parent involvement during high school had a significant positive impact.

Using data from the 1980 High School and Beyond (HS&B) national survey conducted by the National Center for Educational Statistics, this report describes and analyzes the relationship between high school student achievement, and characteristics of the student's family, particularly SES. Achievement is defined as enrollment in postsecondary education and attainment of a college degree.

The influence of family SES on student achievement is well documented: The higher the family income and educational level, the more likely students are to complete high school and enroll in and complete postsecondary education. In her analysis, Eagle examines this relationship more closely, using data on 11,227 HS&B students who were seniors in 1980 and who participated in the 1986 follow-up survey.

SES Effects

Because SES is a composite of five different family characteristics (mother's education, father's education, family income, father's occupational status, and number of certain major possessions such as automobiles and appliances), Eagle first looked at whether all five were associated with higher achievement. She found that "students' educational attainment was strongly associated with all five indicators in the SES composite." (p.3)

Family Background

Next, Eagle examined five other characteristics of students' family background: family composition (number of original parents), parent involvement during high school, parents' reading to the student in early childhood, mother's employment status, and having a special place at home to study. Of these five, the only ones significantly related to student achievement were, from least to most impact: a place to study, family reading, and parent involvement during high school (defined as: frequency of talking to teachers, parent involvement in planning for post-high school activities, and parent monitoring of school work).

"Three everyday interactions between parents and their high school-aged children have a powerful effect on whether students go on to postsecondary education: talking together, planning for post-high school activities, and monitoring school work.

The chart below shows a direct and positive relationship between level of parent involvement and level of student achievement:

Students' highest level of Education:	Parents Highly Involved during HS	Parents Moderately Involved during HS	Parents Not Very Involved during HS
HS Diploma	20%	32%	43%
Some Post-Sec Ed	53	51	48
BA or BS degree	27	17	8

Parent involvement during high school was defined as: frequency of talking to teachers, involvement in planning for post-high school activities, and monitoring of school work.

SES vs. Family Background

Next, Eagle addresses whether advantageous home environments are more common in high-SES homes; that is, are students from high-SES families more likely to have been read to in early childhood, to have a place set aside to study, and to have parents who were involved during high school, than students from low-SES families? The answer is yes; this is, of course, another way to say that high SES is associated with high student achievement.

The question remains: Does high SES alone account for higher achievement, or does family involvement in education have an independent effect? To answer this, Eagle controlled for SES and found three factors that demonstrated a significant impact independent of social background: the possessions index (or level of affluence), students living with neither original parent, and parent involvement during high school. Of these, the most powerful was parent involvement.

Conclusions

While parent affluence and education level are consistently related to their children's educational achievement (that is, students from high-SES families tend to do better than students from low-SES families when both groups of parents are highly involved), "parents of any social class can contribute to their children's postsecondary educational attainment by monitoring educational progress during high school." (p. 12)

See also: Fehrmann et al., Snow, Ziegler.

"Parents of any social class can contribute to their children's postsecondary educational attainment by monitoring educational progress during high school."

Epstein, Joyce L.
"Effects on Student Achievement of Teachers' Practices of Parental Involvement"
Advances in Reading/Language Research, Vol.5, (Greenwich, CT: JAI Press, 1991), pp.261-276

SUMMARY: In a study of student achievement in the classrooms of 14 elementary school teachers who used varying techniques to involve parents in learning activities at home, the author finds a positive and significant effect on student reading achievement.

This study analyzes data from 293 third- and fifth-grade students in 14 classrooms in Baltimore, who took the California Achievement Test (CAT) in the fall, then again in the spring, of the 1980-81 school year. Their teachers were classified into three categories: (1) those who reported frequent use of parent involvement in learning activities at home, or "confirmed leaders," (2) those who were infrequent users, and (3) "confirmed nonusers." These reports were confirmed by their school principals.

Findings

Epstein performed multiple-regression analysis to determine the relative effects of student and family background (sex, race, parent education, fall test scores), teacher quality and leadership in parent involvement, parent reactions (rating of quality of homework assignments and requests), and student effort (quality of homework completed). Comparing spring scores to fall, Epstein found that "teacher leadership in parent involvement in learning activities at home positively and significantly influences change in reading achievement." (p.266)

In addition, parents who reported that they learned more during the year than they previously knew about their child's instructional program, as a result of improved communication with teacher, had a positive influence on their children's reading achievement, as did parents with a higher educational background "who usually help their children." Thus we see that gains come not only for children whose parents make a regular practice of helping them, but also for children whose parents have been encouraged by their teachers to help them.

Epstein did not find a similar relationship for math achievement. In her discussion of the differences of the impact of parent involvement on math versus reading, she provides several explanations:

- Principals encourage teachers to initiate parent involvement in reading activities more than in any other subject.
- Teachers report that reading activities are their most frequently used and most satisfying parent involvement practice.
- Parents are given little guidance on how to help their children with math at home, and may feel inadequate in their knowledge, especially at the fifth-grade level.

"Teacher leadership in parent involvement in learning activities at home positively and significantly influences change in reading achievement."

Gains come not only for children whose parents make a regular practice of helping them, but also for children whose parents have been encouraged by their teachers to help them.

"Parents are one available but un-tapped and un-directed resource that teachers can mobilize to help more children master and maintain needed skills for school...this requires teachers' leadership in organizing, evaluating, and continually building their parent involvement practices."

For parent practices at home to have significant impact on math achievement, teachers may need to give more help to parents of older children so that they understand how to assist, guide and monitor their children's math homework.

Conclusions

Teachers' leadership in involving parents to work with their children at home makes a strong positive contribution to reading achievement, even after teacher quality, students' fall scores, parent education, parent understanding of the school program, and the quality of student homework are taken into account. "Parents are one available but un-tapped and undirected resource that teachers can mobilize to help more children master and maintain needed skills for school...this requires teachers' leadership in organizing, evaluating, and continually building their parent involvement practices." (p.274)

See also: Clark (1993), Dauber and Epstein, Gordon and Olmsted, Leler.

Fehrmann, Paul G., Timothy Z. Keith, and Thomas M. Reimers   EJ362 960
"Home Influence on School Learning: Direct and Indirect Effects of Parental
Involvement on High School Grades"
Journal of Educational Research, *Vol.80, No.6, August 1987, pp. 330-337*

SUMMARY: This analysis of the 1980 High School and Beyond (HS&B) study data on 28,000 high school seniors finds a positive effect on grades if parents are involved in their children's academic and social lives.

These three researchers from the University of Iowa examined the data from the 1980 HS&B longitudinal study, which contains responses from 28,051 high school seniors, to determine what variables that can be controlled by teachers, parents and students have the greatest effect on student grades. Using path analysis, the study also attempted to determine the direct effects of parent involvement on grades, and to determine the extent of indirect effects of parent involvement through homework and TV watching.

The primary variables of concern were parent involvement, grades, TV time, and time spent on homework. The path analysis then looked at the relationships among these variables and background variables (intellectual ability, ethnicity, family background, and gender).

"Parents might well help their high school children achieve higher grades through monitoring (their) daily activities, by keeping close track of how they are doing in school, and by working closely with the students concerning planning for post-high school pursuits."

Findings

As might be expected, the strongest direct relationship was between intellectual ability and grades (.347). Other strong effects, however, were parent involvement (.129), and time spent on homework (.186). Interestingly, time spent watching TV did not appear to be significant (-.049).

The direct effects of gender and ethnicity on TV time were negligible. Higher ability, non-White ethnicity, higher socioeconomic status (SES), and female gender are all associated with spending more time on homework. Parent involvement appears to be greater in non-White families, and high-SES parents appear to be more involved than low-SES families. Also, parents of girls appeared to be more involved than parents of boys.

Conclusions

Parent involvement has an important, direct effect on high school grades. Contrary to the authors' expectations, however, its indirect effect through monitoring time spent on homework and watching TV was not significant. "Parents might well help their high school children achieve higher grades through monitoring [their] daily activities, by keeping close track of how they are doing in school, and by working closely with the students concerning planning for post-high school pursuits."

See also: Benson et al., Eagle, Stevenson and Baker.

For most districts where parent involvement was 'pro forma' and consisted either of filling out a questionnaire or attending large group meetings, the achievement of the pupils was similar, but less than the achievement in the district where parents participated in deciding what was taught and had responsibility for working with the teachers and children."

Gillum, Ronald M.   ED 144 007
"The Effects of Parent Involvement on Student Achievement in Three Michigan Performance Contracting Programs"
Paper presented at the American Education Research Association Annual Meeting, NY, April 1977

SUMMARY: This study of three Michigan school districts that involved parents in performance contracts to improve the reading skills of low-income elementary school children, finds that the district with the most comprehensive parent program scored the greatest gains.

In 1972, the Michigan legislature authorized funds for school districts to conduct performance contracts to improve reading skills in local schools. Three school districts developed programs with parent involvement components.

This study tried to determine if participating students had higher reading achievement than other students, and if there was a significant difference in reading achievement among the three performance-contracting programs. Then it compared the three contracts to determine if differences in parent involvement features accounted for differences in reading achievement.

Nearly 2,000 disadvantaged students in second through sixth grades in 12 schools were tested at the beginning and end of the school year on the Stanford Achievement and the Metropolitan Achievement Tests. The later scores were then compared with national norm tables to determine if student achievement was greater than would have been expected from their earlier scores. Averages were computed for each of the three districts.

The school districts let performance contracts to private organizations, who designed and conducted special reading programs. The amount of pay they received was based on a sliding scale and adjusted according to the gains students made on standardized tests.

Findings

Parent involvement in each of the districts varied widely. District A conducted a community information program for parents and citizens. Each participating school principal held at least four informational meetings during the school year. District B only held an open house at the beginning of the year and presented demonstrations of the program at a PTA meeting. District C built an intensive in-service training program for administrators, parents and teachers into its contract. Forty parent leaders received training, then conducted sessions for other parents on their child's educational program, cooperation at the school, and on reinforcing the program at home. In addition, both parents and schools received incentive vouchers redeemable for educational materials, and parents received stipends for attending meetings.

In all three districts, the participating students achieved significantly higher scores in reading than was expected; but in District C, where parent involvement was the highest, students scored, on the average, considerably higher than those in the other two districts. The program design was nearly identical in all three districts; the only major difference among them were the parent involvement components.

Conclusion

"For most districts where parent involvement was 'pro forma' and consisted either of filling out a questionnaire or attending large group meetings, the achievement of the pupils was similar, but less than the achievement in the district where parents participated in deciding what was taught and had responsibility for working with the teachers and children."

See also: Armor, Comer, Gordon, Mowry, Swap.

> "Whatever discrepancies may in fact exist between dimensions of minority children's home and school experiences, important areas of compatibility also exist, which if explored and exploited, could lead to substantial improvement in minority children's school achievement."

Goldenburg, Claude N.   *EJ 358 789*
"Low-Income Hispanic Parents' Contributions to Their First-Grade Children's Word Recognition Skills"
Anthropology and Education Quarterly, *Vol. 18, 1987, pp. 149-179*

SUMMARY: This article investigates the role nine Hispanic families played in developing the word-recognition skills of their first-grade children. Despite their low education and income, all the parents who participated were both capable of helping their children and willing to do so. In two cases, the parents made a dramatic difference in their children's achievement.

Most research has attempted to explain the low achievement of minority children by invoking one of these two explanations:

- **cultural deprivation:** minority children come to school socially and academically ill-prepared, only to fall progressively further behind their higher status classmates, or
- **cultural incompatibility:** the skills, strengths and values of minority children and their families do not match those of the mainstream Anglo-American culture.

The central theme of this article is that "whatever discrepancies may in fact exist between dimensions of minority children's home and school experiences, important areas of compatibility also exist, which if explored and exploited, could lead to substantial improvement in minority children's school achievement." (p.151)

The author conducted nine case studies of low-income, Hispanic families with little English proficiency, beginning when the children were in kindergarten and ending at the close of first grade. Of the fifteen parents, all born in other countries, only two had been educated beyond the sixth grade.

Information was collected from direct observation at home and school, interviews with parents and teachers, teacher rating scales, student testing, and conversations with the children. Interviews with parents were conducted at home, in Spanish, and included questions about how the family fostered their children's learning, such as:

> After Freddy's parents came to school, his teacher said, "now everything I give him he produces perfectly well. It's a whole new Freddy."

- Amount of reading done at home and the availability of materials to read
- Attitudes about the importance of education
- Involvement with children's learning, particularly reading
- The general learning environment (e.g. conversations, family TV watching, emphasis on homework)
- Contacts with the teacher and the school, and willingness to become more involved in their children's learning.

The interviewer also asked parents about their children's performance in school, and their educational hopes and expectations for their children. Parents expected average to good school performance, and expressed the hope that their children would go "as far as possible."

Findings

When tested, the nine children fell into two distinct groups. The four "successful" ones were reading at grade level, and the five "unsuccessful" ones were substantially below. Although the attitudes and behaviors of the two groups of families, at least in terms of their reading habits and expectations for achievement, were the same, "...some parents had a pronounced effect on their children's reading achievement. In two cases, children's...reading success can be traced directly to parental help."

In both of those cases, parents took direct action to help their children learn to read. Freddy, who was falling substantially behind his classmates, made a dramatic turn-around after both of his parents met with the teacher. After that meeting, his mother came in every day during reading hour. According to the teacher, "now everything I give him he produces perfectly well. It's a whole new Freddy."

Elena's mother, although barely literate, took the initiative to teach her daughter to read, with no prompting from the teacher. From the start of first grade, she taught Elena the sounds and names of the letters, had her copy letters and words, and write words from dictation. Although Elena had some learning difficulties, she was able to keep up with the class.

Yet all the parents were as willing as Freddy's and Elena's to help their children succeed. "If parents did not help their children any more than they did, it was not because they lacked the ability or the interest in their children's education. It was because they either did not perceive a clear need to intervene in what is generally considered to be the school's domain, or because they were uncertain as to what they could do to help their children learn to read." (p.175) Parents can make important contributions to their children's literacy. They can teach their children directly, helping to sound out letters and words; they can read to their children and play letter or word games; and they can encourage their children to tell stories or read aloud.

Conclusion

"Parents represent a vast potential resource in the effort to improve achievement among minority children....Parents of minority children are highly motivated to help their children succeed, and they are very interested in having their children share these values of success through education--at least when their children are in the very early stages of schooling." (p.176) The question for schools, the author asserts, is how to capitalize on this motivation and on the opportunities parents offer to help improve their children's achievement.

See also: Caplan et al., Clark (1993), Wong Fillmore.

"If parents did not help their children any more than they did, it was not because they lacked the ability or the interest in their children's education. It was because they either did not perceive a clear need to intervene in what is generally considered to be the school's domain, or because they were uncertain as to what they could do to help their children learn to read."

Goodson, Barbara D. and Robert D. Hess   ED 136 967
"Parents as Teachers of Young Children: An Evaluative Review of Some Contemporary Concepts and Programs"
Bureau of Educational Personnel Development, DHEW, Office of Education, Washington, DC, May 1975

SUMMARY: This research reviews evaluations of 29 preschool programs for disadvantaged children to determine what effect their various parent-training features have on short and long-term gains in achievement, and discovers that programs are successful regardless of how parent involvement is organized.

This review, which was sponsored by the Department of Health, Education and Welfare, had three objectives:

- To identify categories of parent involvement in early education
- To describe 29 programs that use parent involvement
- To summarize the studies evaluating the programs' effectiveness.

The researchers interviewed project directors and reviewed program evaluations to obtain their data. Although the authors did not visit any of the programs, they described them all at some length. Every program trained parents in how to prepare their preschool children for school. Each was rated according to four criteria:

1. **The parent component:** the level of intensity of the training, from home visits only, through parent classes plus preschool classes for children
2. **The content:** Verbal, sensory-motor, general cognitive, and child development principles
3. **Teacher/parent ratio:** One-to-one, small groups, or one large group
4. **The structure:** Whether training is specific or general, whether the program structure is highly organized or unplanned.

Criteria evaluating the effectiveness of the programs were: (1)immediate advantages on intelligence tests, (2)long-term advantages on intelligence or achievement tests, (3)advantage of program children in school performance, all compared to children in a matched control group.

> "As a group, the programs consistently produced significant immediate gains in children's IQ scores, seemed to show long-term effects on children's IQ and their school performance, and seemed to alter in a positive direction the teaching behavior of parents." (p.233)

Findings

"As a group, the programs consistently produced significant immediate gains in children's IQ scores, seemed to show long-term effects on children's IQ and their school performance, and seemed to alter in a positive direction the teaching behavior of parents." (p.233)

Although some programs were more effective than others, there was no clear relationship between program design and outcome. The authors do not feel this means that program design is unimportant, but speculate that factors other than those measured influenced effectiveness.

Conclusion

The follow-up data suggest that preschool programs which train parents as teachersof their own children may be more successful in producing lasting effects...than preschool programs without parent participation." (p. 214).

Goodson and Hess attribute the success of these programs to an increase in parents' awareness of their influence on their child's behavior, a more systematic focus on parent/child interaction in educational activities, an increase in verbal interaction, and an increase in parent responsiveness to the child.

See also: Bronfenbrenner, Guinagh and Gordon, Lazar and Darlington, Mowry, Radin.

The success of these programs can be attributed to an increase in parents' awareness of their influence on their child's behavior, a more systematic focus on parent/child interaction in educational activities, an increase in verbal interaction, and an increase in parent responsiveness to the child.

"In the parent impact model, the family learns to deal with agencies as they are; in the school (or agency) impact model, the goal of parent involvement is to change the agency, then make it more responsive to the family as it is."

"Programs dealing directly with the family, especially preschool programs, but also school programs, affect in a positive fashion the learning and development of the child. They may be doing this because they are focussing on the family as a learning environment rather than on the child as a learner."

Gordon, Ira
"The Effects of Parent Involvement on Schooling"
In Partners: Parents and Schools, *Brandt, Ronald S., ed., Alexandria, VA: Association for Supervision and Curriculum Development, 1979*

SUMMARY: This review of pertinent research indicates that the more comprehensive and long-lasting the parent involvement, the more effective it is likely to be, not just on children's achievement but on the quality of schools as institutions serving the community.

This study is based on Gordon's work designing early childhood programs such as Follow Through, as well as an extensive review of the research on the effect of parent involvement on student achievement.

Gordon divides parent involvement into three models:

- **Parent Impact Model:** The influence of parents and the home on a child's learning patterns

- **School Impact Model:** Direct parent involvement in the school, from volunteering to serving on governance councils

- **Community Impact Model:** Parent involvement in all possible roles, from teacher at home to active member of the local community.

"In the parent impact model, the family learns to deal with agencies as they are; in the school (or agency) impact model, the goal of parent involvement is to change the agency, then make it more responsive to the family as it is." (p.8)

In the Follow Through program, which is a community impact model, parents play six critical roles: classroom volunteer, paraprofessional, teacher at home, adult educator, adult learner, and decision maker. These roles, which Gordon imagines as spokes on a wheel, each as necessary as the next, will influence not only the parents' behavior, but also change the community agencies with which they interact. For the wheel to turn effectively, parents must play all the roles.

Findings

Most of the research has centered on parent intervention programs at the preschool level, and the evidence is consistently positive that there are significant, long-term effects. Children whose families participate do better than comparable children for as long as ten years after the programs end.

Parent impact programs for school-aged children have not been researched as thoroughly, but the data show that the quantity of home visits is the most important aspect of these programs. They are most effective when carefully planned, last at least a year, have an educational focus, and include as their major delivery system parents working at home with their children.

Gordon found almost no research on the effect of the school impact model on student achievement, partially because it is much more difficult to study.

For the community impact model, evaluation studies of Follow Through and related programs indicate that the effect on achievement of those with well-developed parent components is strong and positive. Children whose parents are directly (rather than indirectly) involved over a period of years, beginning in preschool, score higher on achievement tests than other children.

Conclusion

Gordon concludes that the more comprehensive and long-lasting the parent involvement, in all roles rather than concentrated in one or two, the more effective it is likely to be. Furthermore, the effects are not evident just in children's achievement but in the quality of schools as institutions serving the community.

"Programs dealing directly with the family, especially preschool programs, but also school programs, affect in a positive fashion the learning and development of the child. They may be doing this because they are focussing on the family as a learning environment rather than on the child as a learner." (p. 16)

See also: Bronfenbrenner, Cummins, Guinagh and Gordon, Sattes, Swap, Ziegler.

Gordon concludes that the more comprehensive and long-lasting the parent involvement, in all roles rather than concentrated in one or two, the more effective it is likely to be.

Gotts, Edward Earl
"HOPE, Preschool to Graduation: Contributions to Parenting and School-Family Relations Theory and Practice"
Appalachia Educational Laboratory, Charleston, WV, February 1989

"Treatments that had registered primarily on the child (i.e. TV and group experience) tended to wash out over time; the effect of home visitation, which was jointly directed toward parents and children, persisted over time."

Improved school-family relations seem to help children be more receptive to learn-ing and, consequently, to perform better in school.

SUMMARY: This extensive retrospective study of the HOPE Preschool Program looks at the long-term effects of a home enrichment strategy designed to reach rural families through television, weekly mobile classroom experiences, and home visits. The experimental group that received home visits in addition to the other components showed positive benefits through high school; grade-level promotions and high school graduation rates were 50 percent higher than for the control group.

The Home-Oriented Preschool Program (HOPE), operated by the Ap-palachia Educational Laboratory from 1968-1971, served three- to five-year-old children in a rural four-county area in West Virginia. The program consisted of three components: daily television lessons, a week-ly group experience for children in a mobile classroom, and in some cases, weekly home visits by paraprofessionals using printed materials corresponding to the TV lessons.

A follow-up study was begun in 1978, comparing the experiences of the HOPE children with a control group. The final phase of the study was conducted in 1985-1988, when the HOPE participants were enrolled in, or graduated from, high school. Gotts describes the scope of this study as "immense," tracking 212 families with 342 children from preschool through high school, and using highly complex methodology to align and interpret different types of data, including 72 individual variables derived from parent and child interviews, school behavior checklists, school records, and school-family relations interviews.

Short-term Findings

- HOPE "was an effective program that resulted in immediate gains for children who were exposed to any of the program com-ponents, including television by itself."

- During preschool, the HOPE children showed gains in early concept development, perceptual-motor function, vocabulary and psycholinguistic abilities.

- Children whose families received weekly home visits showed greater gains than the TV-only children, and children who had participated in the weekly classes showed improved curiosity and social interaction.

- The early conceptual development of the HOPE children equalled or exceeded those of similar children in a kindergarten comparison group, yet cost analysis showed that HOPE costs were about half those for traditional kindergarten.

- During the primary grades, the HOPE children continued to show positive effects compared to the control group: improved attendance, higher grades, improved scores on tests of achievement and ability.

Long-term Findings

- By the time the HOPE children were in primary school, those who had experienced only the TV component did not show gains past the second grade, while those who had also attended the weekly classes did not show gains after the first few years.

- The only component that registered long-term effects (10-12 years) was the home-visit group.

- Although extensive analysis revealed that program benefits differed somewhat for boys and girls, each sex showed significant academic gains. In addition, HOPE appeared to prevent "unfavorable emotional patterns and personality characteristics in boys and enhanced the self-concepts of girls." (p.267)

- Favorable effects of the program on school-family relations were still apparent 12-14 years after it ended. HOPE parents learned to be advocates for their children, to push the school into offering a better education, and to judge school staff by how well they worked with parents to help their children. These improved school-family relations seem to help children be more receptive to learning and, consequently, to perform better in school.

Conclusion

"Treatments that had registered primarily on the child (i.e. TV and group experience) tended to wash out over time; the effect of home visitation, which was jointly directed toward parents and children, persisted over time. This persistence is attributed to enhanced skills in the parents that could be used continually throughout the years of their children's development." (p.264)

See also: Bronfenbrenner, Guinagh and Gordon, Lazar, Schweinhart and Weikart.

Favorable effects of the program on school-family relations were still apparent 12-14 years after it ended. HOPE parents learned to be advocates for their children, to push the school into offering a better education, and to judge school staff by how well they worked with parents to help their children.

"The results indicate...clear, lasting school achievement and performance effects for children who were in the parent education program with their parents for two or three consecutive years ending when they were two- or three-years-old."

The lasting effects on the children, Guinagh and Gordon speculate, are attributable to the impact of the program on the family.

Guinagh, Barry and Ira Gordon   ED 135 469
"School Performance as a Function of Early Stimulation"
Florida University at Gainesville, Institute for Development of Human Resources, December 1976

SUMMARY: This longitudinal study of an early childhood parent-education project training low-income mothers to use learning materials at home produced significant advances in reading and math tests when the children entered school. These advantages were maintained into the fourth grade.

The authors tracked 91 representative graduates of parent education projects in 12 Florida counties to determine if the program produced lasting effects on school performance and home-school relations. They compared assignments to special education programs as well as reading and math scores for up to six years following the end of the program for three groups of children: those involved for two-to-three years, beginning when the child was under one-year-old; those involved for one year; and those in a control group. All were randomly assigned to these groups at entry into the program.

The parent program consisted of home visits twice every three weeks by a paraprofessional, each lasting about an hour, during which mothers were shown how to use materials in learning activities with their children at home. The program ended on the child's third birthday.

Findings

When tested at the beginning of first grade, three years after finishing the early-education program, and again during third grade, the two treatment groups had many fewer assignments to special education classes (under five percent, as compared to 25 percent for the control group), and the two-to-three year group had significantly higher scores on reading and math tests than the control group.

Conclusion

"Results indicate...clear, lasting school achievement and performance effects for children who were in the parent education program with their parents for two or three consecutive years ending when they were two- or three-years-old." (p.45) This effect persisted up to six years after the end of the program, both in achievement test scores and assignments to special education. These lasting effects, Guinagh and Gordon speculate, are attributable to the impact of the program on the family.

Researchers are encouraged that a home visit program using paraprofessionals can be sustained for two-to-three years, using simple materials, and can lead to gains that last through the fourth grade.

See also: Bronfenbrenner, Gotts, Lazar and Darlington, Leler.

Irvine, David J.   ED 176 893
"Parent Involvement Affects Children's Cognitive Growth"
University of the State of New York, State Education Department, Division of
Research, Albany, August 1979

SUMMARY: This study of an experimental pre-kindergarten program for disadvantaged children in New York State found that parent involvement had a highly significant effect on reasoning, verbal concepts, and school-related skills.

Irvine designed the analysis to determine whether the performance of four-year-old children on each of three measures of cognitive achievement was related to the amount of time their parents were involved in the experimental program. Controls were introduced to test whether the involvement was actually related to achievement, rather than to other factors, such as levels of family education and income, or children's age and previous performance.

Parent involvement included school visits, home visits by school personnel, meetings, employment in the program, and incidental contacts. Five levels of involvement were determined according to the number of hours the parents were involved over the school year (0, 50, 100, 150, or 200 hours).

Findings

For general reasoning, as measured by the Walker Readiness Test for Disadvantaged Children, the author found that parent involvement had a "highly significant effect." Children's scores varied directly with the number of hours their parents were involved, controlling for all other factors.

For school-related knowledge and skills, as measured by the Cooperative Preschool Inventory, Irvine also found that parent involvement had a highly significant effect, controlling for other factors.

For knowledge of verbal concepts, as measured by the Peabody Picture Vocabulary Test, there was a highly significant relationship between parent involvement and achievement, with the *greatest* effect for children who had started out with lowest scores.

Conclusion

Irvine found that "the children who tended to score highest on three measures of cognitive development were those whose parents spent the most time participating in activities related to the program or the school." (p.3) "Parent involvement appears to affect general reasoning and school-related knowledge and skills regardless of the child's age, mother's education, family income, or level of performance at the beginning of pre-kindergarten." (p.12)

Children's readiness scores varied directly with the number of hours their parents were involved, controlling for all other factors.

There was a highly significant relationship between parent involvement and verbal achievement, with the greatest effect for children who had started out with lowest scores.

This table shows the direct, positive relationship between level of parent involvement and degree of student achievement:

"Finding a highly significant effect of parent involvement on three different dimensions of cognitive development is a striking result." (p.9)

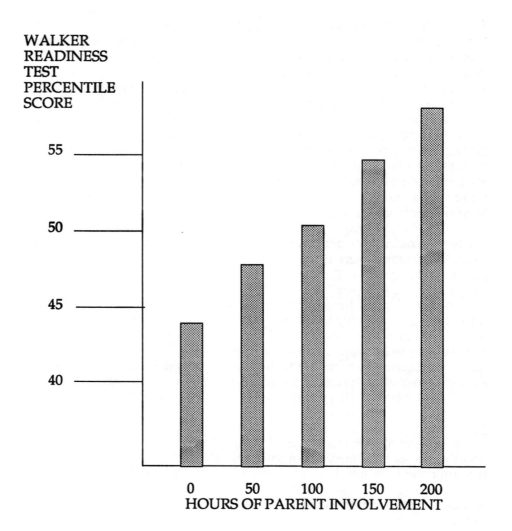

See also: Goodson and Hess, Mowry, Radin, Reynolds, Schweinhart and Weickart.

Kellaghan, Thomas, Kathryn Sloane, Benjamin Alvarez, and Benjamin S. Bloom
The Home Environment & School Learning: Promoting Parental Involvement in the Education of Children
(San Francisco: Jossey-Bass, Inc., 1993)

SUMMARY: This book reviews a large body of research and finds that the home environment is a powerful factor in determining the academic success of students--their level of achievement, their interest in learning, and the years of schooling they will complete. The authors also outline a program parents can use at home to support their children's scholastic development.

Reviewing some 300 studies on home-school relations, the authors find that, taken together, they confirm that the home is central to children's learning and progress in school. In addition, they consider the historical, social and demographic circumstances that have resulted in changing family roles and structures -- as well as a serious discontinuity between home and school for many children.

As the traditional role of the family as a unit of economic production has diminished, the extent of formal schooling has expanded. Yet families still make critical contributions to their children's education. From birth to age 18, children spend only about 13 percent of their waking hours in school; parents continue to have major responsibility for the huge remainder of their children's time. We cannot, the authors suggest, rely on schools alone to prepare young people to participate in modern society. "It seems most unlikely that a significant improvement in the quality of education for all students can be achieved without active support from other quarters...particularly families." (p.8)

"It seems most unlikely that a significant improvement in the quality of education for all students can be achieved without active support from other quarters... particularly families."

Findings

Ideally, home and school should play complementary, mutually reinforcing roles in education, but major differences exist between the two institutions. For children from immigrant and minority families, the discontinuities can be severe. Research studies suggest two ways of dealing with this problem:

- increasing the overlap between home and school
- helping children learn how to apply cognitive and social skills learned at home to activities and tasks at school.

Home "processes" play an important role in children's development: how time and space are organized and used, how parents and children interact and spend time together, and the values that govern the family's choice of things to do. The authors believe that it is these home-process variables, rather than the social or economic status of parents, that determine how well children do at school.

> *"The home environment is a most powerful factor in determining the school learning of students--their level of school achievement, their interest in school learning, and the number of years of schooling they will receive."*

To engage families in their children's education, a number of home intervention programs have been designed and implemented over the past three decades. The authors classify them into three models:

- **The deficit model**: Based on the assumption that many families were unable or unwilling to provide the stimulation or resources necessary to prepare their children for school
- **The difference model**: Recognizing the strengths and knowledge of all parents and helping the child adjust to a "different," though not superior, school environment
- **The empowerment model**: Based on the premise that "the roles of parent and teacher are equal and complementary, sharing the same purpose and characterized by mutual respect, information sharing, and decision making." (p.92)

A Framework for Parent Education

The five home process variables outlined below can be used as a framework for home intervention or parent education programs.

- **Work habits of the family**: A regular family routine and priority given to schoolwork over other activities
- **Academic guidance and support**: The quality of encouragement that parents give to their children's schoolwork
- **Stimulation to explore and discuss ideas and events**: Opportunities to explore ideas, events, and the larger environment
- **Language environment**: Opportunities to develop the correct and effective use of language
- **Academic aspirations and expectations**: Parents' aspirations for their children, their standards for school achievement, and their knowledge of children's school experiences.

Conclusions

The authors draw several conclusions:

- "The home environment is a most powerful factor in determining level of school achievement, interest in school learning, and the number of years of schooling." (p. 144-5)
- When home and school have different approaches to learning, children's achievement may be affected. Both home and school should help children bridge any discontinuities that exist.
- The socioeconomic level or cultural background of the home and family need not determine a child's success in school. What parents do in the home is more critical than their status.
- Parents are in a better position to encourage home-learning activities if they understand what is expected of their child at school and are kept informed of specific steps they can take to support those expectations.

> *"Schools are likely to find rewarding any efforts they make to link home and school, not only in terms of improved student behavior and achievement but also in the support network that a close home-school partnership can provide for their work." (p. 153)*

See also: Clark (1983, 1990), Comer, Cummins, Steinberg et al., Swap, Wong Fillmore.

Lareau, Annette   *EJ 353 123*
"Social Class Differences in Family-School Relationships: the Importance of Cultural Capital"
Sociology of Education, *vol. 60, April 1987, pp. 73-85*

SUMMARY: This study comparing family-school relationships in a middle-class versus a working-class elementary school, finds that the differences in the way parents respond to teacher requests and interact with the school may explain the lower achievement, aspirations, and life prospects for working-class children.

The theory of cultural capital argues that schools draw unevenly on the resources of their students' families. Children from higher social status families enter school familiar with the language, authority structure, and curriculum, an advantage that pays off in academic achievement. Drawing on this notion, Lareau suggests that "class-related cultural factors" influence how parents comply with teachers' requests for parent involvement.

For her intensive study, Lareau picked two elementary schools, one ("Prescott") in a professional, middle-class community in which the majority of parents were college-educated, the other ("Colton") in a working-class community, where most parents were high school graduates or dropouts employed in skilled or semi-skilled occupations. For a six-month period, Lareau visited one first-grade classroom at each school once or twice a week for about two hours. At the end of the school year, she selected six children in each class for further study, a boy and a girl from the high, medium and low reading groups. "To prevent the confounding influence of race," she selected only White children. Lareau interviewed the parents at the beginning and end of second grade, as well as the first- and second-grade teachers, the school principals and a resource specialist.

Findings

"At both schools, the definition of the ideal family-school relationship was the same: a partnership in which family life and school life are integrated." (p.76) As a result, teachers promoted parent involvement in several ways:

- Newsletters invited families to school events
- Teachers encouraged students to bring parents to school events
- Teachers encouraged parents to read to their children and to review and reinforce the material learned in class
- Teachers asked parents to tell them of any concerns about their children

Although teachers and administrators talked about being "partners" with parents, it was clear that they expected parents to defer to them. The requests teachers made of parents did not vary by their social class.

Because middle-class families tended to socialize with other parents in the community, while working-class families tended to see their relatives, "the social networks of the middle-class parents provided them with additional sources of information about their child's school experience; the networks of working-class parents did not."

"*Parents in both communities valued educational success; all wanted their children to do well in school, and all saw themselves as supporting and helping their children achieve success in school. Middle- and working-class parents' aspirations differed only in the level of achievement they hoped their children would attain.*"

In both schools, teachers clearly promoted all the types of teacher-directed parent involvement listed above.

The response parents made to the various teacher requests was much higher at Prescott, the middle-class school, than at Colton. Nearly all the Prescott parents attended parent-teacher conferences, for example, and their attendance at the annual open house was almost three times higher. The difference between the two schools was evident not only in how often parents and teachers interacted. At Colton, the interactions at school events were stiff and awkward; when parents spoke with teachers, the conversation tended to be short, rather formal, and serious. Prescott parents much more readily raised academic concerns and played an active role in reinforcing and monitoring their children's schoolwork.

Influences on Parent Participation

A variety of factors influenced the amount of parent involvement: parents' educational level, their view of the appropriate division of labor between teachers and parents, the information they received about their children's schooling, and the time, money and other material resources available to them.

Colton parents expressed doubts about their own educational capabilities; as a result, they turned over the responsibility to the teacher. Prescott parents saw themselves as partners with teachers in promoting their children's progress. Furthermore, Colton mothers had to make complicated arrangements for transportation and child care to attend school events, while Prescott parents had two cars, greater flexibility in their work schedules, and funds to hire household help.

There were similar differences in the information parents were able to obtain about their children's experience in school. Because middle-class Prescott families tended to socialize with other parents in the school community, they knew what was going on: the names of the teachers, which children were doing well, and who was receiving special services. Colton parents tended to socialize with relatives and had little or no contact with other parents. In other words, "the social networks of the middle-class parents provided them with additional sources of information about their child's school experience; the networks of working-class parents did not." (p.81)

Implications

At both schools, teachers interpreted parent response as a reflection of the value parents placed on their children's of success. Interviews and observations of parents told a different story: "Parents in both communities valued educational success; all wanted their children to do well in school, and all saw themselves as supporting and helping their children achieve success in school. Middle- and working-class parents' aspirations differed only in the level of achievement they hoped their children would attain." (p.81) Middle-class culture furthers connections between home and school, reinforcing teachers' positive attitudes toward their children, while working-class culture emphasizes separation, lowering teachers' expectations for these children.

Conclusion

In her discussion, Lareau makes a key point: if the schools were to promote a different type of family-school relationship, middle-class culture might not provide such an advantage. The profitability of middle-class arrangements does not come from their superiority; it derives from the school's definition of the proper family-school relationship. "For most children (but not all), social class is a major predictor of educational and occupational achievement. Schools...play a crucial role in this process of social reproduction; they sort students into social categories that award credentials and opportunities for mobility."

See also: Baker and Stevenson, Dornbusch, Wong Fillmore.

Middle-class culture furthers connections between home and school, reinforcing teachers' positive attitudes toward their children, while working-class culture emphasizes separation, lowering teachers' expectations for these children.

Early-education programs significantly reduced the number of children assigned to special-education classes or retained in grade, regardless of their initial abilities or home background, and increased children's scores on fourth-grade math and readiness tests.

Three of the five program characteristics most highly associated with effectiveness were related to parent involvement: home visits, program goals for parents, and parent involvement.

Lazar, Irving and Richard B. Darlington   ED 175 523
"Summary: Lasting Effects After Preschool"
Consortium for Longitudinal Studies, Cornell University, 1978

SUMMARY: This long-term study of 11 early-childhood projects involving parents shows that participating children performed better in school and had significantly fewer assignments to special-education classes or grade retentions than control-group children for many years after they completed the projects.

This report is a summary analysis of the lasting effects of preschool intervention projects for predominantly Black, low-income children. Data on more than 2,000 children were gathered from 11 carefully designed projects conducted around the country during the 1960s. Follow-up data were collected on both subject and control children in 1976-77 and compared, to determine if the preschool projects still had measurable effects on school performance.

The programs studied fall into three categories:

1. **Center-based,** with a nursery school-type program in which parents visited and were observed

2. **Home-based,** with educational efforts directed toward training the mother as a major influence in the child's life

3. **Combined home/center,** combining a nursery school program with periodic home visits.

Findings

The researchers found that, both individually and as a group, the programs had lasting effects on the children's performance in school. Early-education programs significantly reduced the number of children assigned to special education classes or retained in grade, regardless of their initial abilities or home background, and increased children's scores on fourth-grade math and readiness tests. Graduates of all the projects maintained higher IQ scores 10-15 years later. In addition, children who attended preschool were more likely to have attitudes positively related to achievement, and their mothers were more likely to have higher aspirations for them.

Conclusion

Three of the five program characteristics most highly associated with effectiveness were related to parent involvement: home visits, program goals for parents, and parent involvement. "Together they suggested that the most effective programs involved one instructor working with an infant or toddler and his/her parent in the home." (p.39)

Lazar and Darlington found all the program designs to be about equally effective with all types of children, whether high or low IQ, male or female, educated or uneducated parents. Although parent involvement was not isolated and separately measured as a factor in program effectiveness (largely because there was substantial parent involvement in all the programs studied), Lazar and Darlington feel that it is an integral part of a "cluster" of factors essential to program success. They also caution that to be effective, a program must be well designed.

See also: Bronfenbrenner, Goodson and Hess, Gotts, Schweinhart and Weikart.

"The most effective programs involved one instructor working with an infant or toddler and his/her parent in the home."

Leler, Hazel
"Parent Education and Involvement in Relation to the Schools and to Parents of School-Aged Children"
In Parent Education and Public Policy, *Haskins and Adams, Norwood, NJ: Ablex Publishing Co., 1987*

SUMMARY: This extensive and rigorous review of 48 studies of educational programs with parent involvement finds that the fuller the participation of parents, the more effective the results.

In this review, largely of unpublished studies or doctoral dissertations, the author analyzes the effects of various parent-education programs on student achievement. The studies are classified according to Ira Gordon's three models of parent involvement, described in some detail, and their effects summarized at the end of each section.

Findings

Parent Impact Model: Most of the studies reviewed looked at the effects of training parents to help their children by reinforcing at home what they were learning at school. Of the 18 studies in this group, 13 showed positive effects on one or more variables. None showed any negative results.

A second group of studies looked at "parenting" programs such as Parent Effectiveness Training. Eight of 12 studies showed positive effects on achievement for students whose parents participated in workshops to improve their child-rearing skills. Again, none had any negative results.

Of the programs that did not show significant results, Leler observes that they were not particularly well designed, and the materials contained jargon that parents might not understand.

School Impact Model: These very few studies examined the experience of involving parents in decision-making roles. They found that educators, parents, administrators, and school board members all would like more parent impact on decision making. There were no studies that looked at the effect of this model on achievement.

Community Impact Model: The primary examples of this model lie in the Parent Education Follow Through Program developed by Ira Gordon and his associates, and several sites of a bilingual Head Start program. In both programs, parents were involved in all possible roles, from home tutoring to program management. All studies in this category produced highly positive results on student achievement. In the bilingual program, evaluation data show that students not only performed at up to twice the levels of matched comparison groups, but approached or surpassed national norms after one or more years.

In the bilingual Head Start program, evaluation data show that students not only performed at up to twice the levels of matched comparison groups, but approached or surpassed national norms after one or more years.

"The fuller the participation of parents, the more effective the results obtained."

Conclusion

The studies summarized "seem to indicate that the fuller the participation of parents, the more effective the results obtained." (p.173) Particularly promising are the approaches where parents have a definite role in decision making.

The author concludes that the approaches with the most potential are those where parents play a variety of roles, including decision making, and where there is a structured program of training for both parents and school personnel.

See also: Cummins, Gordon, Guinagh and Gordon, Olmsted and Rubin, Simich-Dudgeon.

The approaches with the most potential are those where parents play a variety of roles, including decision making, and where there is a structured program of training for both parents and school personnel.

McDill, Edward L, Leo Rigsby, and Edmond Meyers   ED 030 205
"Educational Climates of High Schools: Their Effects and Sources"
Johns Hopkins University Center for the Study of Social Organization of Schools, Baltimore, April 1969

SUMMARY: **In this large nationwide study, parent involvement was found to be the** *critical* **factor in the achievement and aspirations of high school students.**

This large-scale study sponsored by the U. S. Office of Education explored three problems: identification of different dimensions of education and social climates of high schools, their relative effect on academic performance and college plans of students, and the relationship between sources of climate on the achievement and college plans of students.

The researchers selected a diverse sample of twenty public high schools in eight states, then sent questionnaires to over 20,000 students, 1,000 faculty members, and all 20 principals. Two academic tests were administered to all the students in the schools, the Aptitude for Abstract Reasoning and the Achievement in Math tests from Project TALENT.

Parent involvement in the high school was identified as a "climate source variable" and correlated with achievement measures and college plans. The level of parent involvement was determined by faculty responses to three questions: are parents apathetic to school policies, do parents seem interested in their children's progress, and do parents often ask for appointments with teachers to discuss their children's schoolwork.

Findings

The authors found that the degree of parental and community interest in quality education is "the critical factor in explaining the impact of the high school environment on the achievement and educational aspirations of students."(p. 27) Not only did parent involvement have a "substantial effect on math achievement and college plans," it also had a significant effect on the achievement and aspirations of students even when controlling for ability and family educational background.

Conclusion

"School and home environments which are mutually reinforcing are likely to achieve greater academic growth of students than those lacking such consistency." (p.29) In conclusion, McDill et al. quote former U.S. Commissioner of Education Harold Howe:

> In all communities--rural and suburban, but especially inner-city--the principal needs to take the initiative in tailoring his school to the character of the community. He needs to solicit parent participation and to help parents understand what kind of contributions they can make. The principal ought to be wel-

The degree of parental and community interest in quality education is "the critical factor in explaining the impact of the high school environment on the achievement and educational aspirations of students."

"School and home environments which are mutually reinforcing are likely to achieve greater academic growth of students than those lacking such consistency."

coming parents and letting them see how the school is run and explain to them its policies and programs. He should at the same time be converting the school into a community resource that offers adults a center for community activities, for instruction in practical subjects as well as leisure-time activities.

See also: Coleman and Hoffer, Phillips, Wagenaar.

"The principal ought to be welcoming parents and letting them see how the school is run and explain to them its policies and programs. He should at the same time be converting the school into a community resource that offers adults a center for community activities, for instruction in practical subjects as well as leisure-time activities."
--Harold Howe

Melnick, Steven A. and Richard Fiene   ED 322 643
"Assessing Parents' Attitudes Toward School Effectiveness"
Paper presented at the Annual Meeting of the American Educational Research Association, Boston, April 16-20, 1990

SUMMARY: Although not documenting a causal relationship, this study of urban elementary school parents suggests that increased parent involvement not only contributes to positive attitudes toward the school, but also to their children's academic performance.

Parents' attitudes toward the schools can be a crucial factor in their children's success in education. In this study, Melnick and Fiene look at parents' relationship with the school to determine:

1. If the frequency of parents' visits to the school and the reasons for the visits make any significant difference in parent attitudes toward the school
2. If parents with more positive attitudes toward the school have children who are performing better than parents with less positive attitudes.

Questionnaires were sent to 4,979 parents of children attending grades K-5 in 11 schools in an urban district. A total of 3,328 were completed and returned, representing a response rate of 67 percent. The parents responding were 67 percent Black, 19 percent White, and 11 percent Hispanic. The instrument used was the Parent Attitude Toward School Effectiveness Survey (PATSE), which uses a five-point Likert rating scale (5=strongly agree to 1=strongly disagree) to represent attitudes toward six aspects of school effectiveness:

- Close home-school relations
- Clear school mission
- High expectations for students
- Safe and orderly environment
- Strong instructional leadership
- Frequent monitoring of student progress

Parents were also asked about the number of visits they made to their child's school and the reasons for the visits:

- To volunteer
- To attend an athletic event
- To attend an academic or cultural event
- To discuss a discipline problem
- To discuss child's progress

Parents were separated into three groups according to the number of visits to the school per year: low (0-1), medium (2-5), and high (6+). To examine the correlation between parent attitudes and student performance, a smaller random sample of 250 students was drawn from the total group. For these students, scores from the Iowa Test of Basic Skills

"Involving parents in substantive ways in their children's schooling has a significant impact on parents' attitudes toward the school. A second finding demonstrates a direct relationship between parents' attitudes toward the school and school achievement." (p. 1)

were collected and matched with the responses of parents whose attitudes fell into the lowest 25 percent and into the highest 25 percent.

Findings

Substantive parent involvement in their children's schooling appears to have a significant relationship to the parents' attitudes toward school effectiveness. Parents who visited their child's school for positive reasons (to volunteer, to attend an academic/cultural event, or to discuss their child's progress) tended to rate the effectiveness of the school higher. Parents who visited the schools for more negative reasons (to discuss discipline problems), or did not visit school at all rated the effectiveness of the school lower on all six effectiveness factors.

Frequency of school visits	Rating of six school effectiveness factors
Low (0-1)	3.54
Medium (2-5)	3.64
High (more than 6)	3.76

The authors also find that parents' attitudes toward school effectiveness are related to student achievement. The achievement scores of children whose parents expressed high regard for the quality of the schools were higher than the scores of children whose parents did not rate the school as high. Three of the factors—high expectations, safe and orderly environment, and frequent monitoring of student progress—showed the strongest relationship to student achievement scores. "Parents who believe that the school has high expectations of their children and frequently monitor their children's progress have children who tend to be higher achievers."

Conclusions

The authors suggest that a "working partnership between parents, teachers, and administrators" may be more significant than traditional parent involvement activities which tend to be separate from day-to-day education in the classroom. (p.7)

They are also careful to point out that while the study does not show a causal relationship, the findings suggest that increased parent involvement not only contributes to positive school perceptions, but is also related to improved academic performance.

See also: Dauber and Epstein, Epstein, Reynolds, Stevenson and Baker.

"The kind of parental involvement needed in public schools is a working partnership of parents, teachers and administrators rather than an intensification of the separate, traditional parental involvement activities." (p. 7)

"Parents did not want to be parent of a 'professional-client' relationship with the school or to be patronized in any way. It would appear...that the manner in which a parental involvement program is introduced to parents may be as important as the program itself." (p.9)

Not only are more children than ever before living with single parents, but more than half of women with young children work outside the home.

Because single mothers, who head the vast majority of single-parent families, have markedly lower family income than married couples, the effects on achievement "probably operate through the lessened family income and beyond that on resources providable to the children by that income.

Milne, Ann M.
"Family Structure and the Achievement of Children"
Education and the American Family, *New York: William J. Weston, ed.,
University Press, pp. 32-65, 1989*

SUMMARY: This review of the literature examines the impact of family structure, specifically the number of parents in a family and whether the mother works outside the home, on children's achievement in school. Although the various findings are complex and mixed, on the whole, what matters is not family structure, but whether parents are able to provide positive educational experiences for their children.

The past twenty years have brought dramatic changes in family structure. Not only are more children than ever before living with single parents, but more than half of women with young children work outside the home. Projections for children born in 1980 are that at least 70 percent will spend some time before they are 17 living with only one parent.

Just as dramatic is the increase in women entering the labor force:

Percentage of Women Working Outside the Home

	1970	1985
Women with no children	42%	48%
With children under 18	40%	61%
With children under 6	30%	53%

To understand the implications these changes hold for children's achievement, Milne reviewed about 60 articles, books and reviews of other research, covering more than a hundred individual studies.

Findings on Single Parent Families

Two major reviews of the research (Shinn, 1978 and Heatherington, Featherman and Camara, 1981), found "that both males and females from single-parent families performed less well than those from two-parent families." (p.39) The overall differences were small, generally less than a year. That is, children from two-parent families tended to be a few months ahead of children from single-parent families in their development.

Next Milne examines whether varying circumstances influence the effects on children.

- **Sex of Parent:** Children living with fathers achieved less well than children living with mothers, although the difference was small.
- **Remarriage:** Children in reconstituted families (i.e. where the custodial parent has a new partner) appear to have lower achievement than children in intact families, but higher than children in single-parent families.
- **Age of Children:** Some studies suggest that the effects of separation are greater for younger children, and decrease as children age; but others find a "lag" in effect, such as a decrease in intelligence at age 12 that was not there at six.
- **Gender of children:** One study found that boys living without fathers scored lower in aptitude and achievement than boys in two-parent homes, and that girls in one-parent families scored higher than girls in two-parent homes. Other studies did not find a clear pattern.
- **Race:** Studies have found contradictory results when comparing Black and White children from single-parent families. The total effects can probably be accounted for by differences in family income rather than race.
- **Socioeconomic Status:** Because single mothers, who head the vast majority of single-parent families, have markedly lower family income than married couples, the effects on achievement "probably operate through the lessened family income and beyond that on resources providable to the children by that income--including a mother who had the option...of staying at home with the child...." (p.45)

Findings on Working Mothers

Reviewing the literature on maternal employment, Milne observes that where effects are found, it is through subgroups defined by race and gender. Because these may work in opposite directions, the effects cancel each other out in studies that do not analyze by subgroups, appearing to show that maternal employment makes no difference.

- When mothers in very-low-income families work, the impact on all their children appears to be beneficial. One study found positive effects for elementary-aged children but negative results for high school students.
- In White, middle-class families, the effects of the mothers' working appear in several studies to be positive for female children but negative for males. Other studies where gender is not separated found negative effects for White elementary-aged children from two-parent families but not from single-parent families, and for White high school students from all families.
- It appears that negative effects of mothers' working result from less time spent with their children, with the greatest detriment for children with more highly educated mothers.

Milne concludes this section with an observation, "time spent with children is not in and of itself critical, but rather the activities that fill that time. While it may be true that the better-educated mother is by nature

Children from two-parent families tended to be a few months ahead of children from single-parent families in their development.

"Time spent with children is not in and of itself critical, but rather the activities that fill that time. While it may be true that the better-educated mother is by nature a more effective teacher of her child, it is becoming more and more obvious that there are processes and environments that parents of any background could provide for their children...."

"Family structures are not inherently good or evil per se; what is important is the ability of the parent(s) to provide proeducational resources for their children--be they financial, material, or experiential."

a more effective teacher of her child, it is becoming more and more obvious that there are processes and environments that parents of any background could provide for their children...." (p.57)

Conclusions

Living in a two-parent household benefits children's achievement. Although some of the differences are small, they all point in the same direction. There appear to be no advantages for children who live in a single-parent household. The evidence is less clear for mothers' working; the negative effects that have been found seem to be related to the circumstances associated with the work. In other words, the educational level of the mother (or caregiver) is critical in determining the effects of the mother's working, while income is critical in determining the impact of the number of parents.

"Family structures are not inherently good or evil per se; what is important is the ability of the parent(s) to provide proeducational resources for their children--be they financial, material, or experiential." (p. 58)

See also: Clark (1983), Scott-Jones (1984), Stevenson and Baker.

Mitrsomwang, Suparvadee and Willis Hawley
"Cultural 'Adaptation' and the Effects of Family Values and Behaviors on the
Academic Achievement and Persistence of Indochinese Students"
Final Report to the Office of Educational Research and Improvement of the U.S.
Department of Education, Grant No. R 117E 00045, 1993

SUMMARY: Examining the experiences and attitudes of Indochinese families, the researchers find that strong family values and behaviors related to education, not just cultural and religious beliefs, had a positive influence on their high school students' performance at school.

Reviewing the literature on socialization and educational achievement of Indochinese students, the researchers suggest that previous research may overemphasize the role of religious beliefs in the formation of values and behavior that affect academic performance. This study explores factors other than religion and philosophy that may have a strong impact on parent's values related to education.

Two types of data are used for this study:

1. Statistical data on student performance (test scores and grades) of Laotian, Cambodian, and Vietnamese 10th- and 11th- graders in the Nashville, Tennessee schools

2. Qualitative/ethnographic information gathered from interviews with families of 12 students, four from each country (two doing well in school and two doing poorly). All families were working-class or low-income, and had two parents and at least one child in addition to the high school student in the sample.

Findings

Mitrsomwang and Hawley find three major influences which have affected significantly the value development of these families:

- Pre-immigration experiences, including the social structure, opportunities for social mobility, exposure to other cultures, and dangerous political situations in their native country
- Immigration experiences, particularly the number of years the family spent in overcrowded camps
- Post-immigration experiences, such as educational and employment opportunities, how parents reacted to U.S. values, and pressures from their own community to maintain cultural traditions.

The most significant finding both confirms and modifies the proposition that parent values and behavior are crucial factors that contribute to student achievement at school. "The stronger the values related to education the parents held, the more developmental and intervention

"The stronger the values related to education the parents held, the more developmental and intervention behaviors the parents performed, and the higher was the children's academic performance."

The presence of these three factors was strongly connected to student achievement:

- *strong, consistent values about the importance of education*
- *willingness to help children and intervene at school*
- *ability to become involved.*

behaviors the parents performed, and the higher was the children's academic performance." (p.46)

Conclusions

The researchers identify three factors that influence the connection between values and behaviors:

- consistency of parents' values on education
- willingness to help children and intervene at school
- ability to perform those behaviors.

In families where all three factors were strong, students were performing well above average in school, but where one or more were weak, students performed less well. Families with strong values about education who did not follow through on intervention behaviors (e.g. contact the school or help their child learn at home) had students with average performance. These parents often had a strong commitment to education and were willing to support their children, but their limited English proficiency and limited information about the educational system hampered them. Families who had weaker values but were actively involved in their child's education also had children with average performance. Children's performance was lowest when families had both weak values and behaviors.

Parents with a strong, consistent commitment to education, who were also willing and able to learn about the schools and become involved, had children whose academic achievement was well above average.

See also: Baker and Stevenson, Caplan et al., Clark (1980, 1990), Wong Fillmore.

Mowry, Charles   ED 080 216
"Investigation of the Effects of Parent Participation in Head Start:
Non-Technical Report"
Department of Health, Education and Welfare, Washington, DC, November
1972

SUMMARY: This report found that Head Start centers with high levels of parent involvement consistently had children who performed higher on standardized tests, parents who were more satisfied, and communities that were more responsive to the disadvantaged, than centers with low parent involvement.

The Head Start program mandates parent involvement in every local project. This study looks at three types:

- Parents as decision makers
- Parents as learners
- Parents as paid employees of Head Start

The effects of parent involvement on four areas of the program were then investigated: quality of the program, change in community institutions, achievement of Head Start children, and attitudes of Head Start parents.

From a ten percent random sample, the researchers selected for study 20 Head Start centers across the United States. They then identified from structured interviews five centers **high** in parent involvement opportunities, five **low** in opportunities, and ten **mixed** in types of opportunities. At each center, approximately 20 parent-child pairs were studied; these were also broken down into high-low categories from questionnaires.

To measure effects on parents, researchers used self-report questionnaires; effects on children were gauged via standardized tests measuring cognitive and intellectual development, school readiness, self-concept and social adjustment. To measure program quality, researchers used staff questionnaires; and for community change, structured group interviews with local citizens and parents.

Findings on Parents and Students

Parents who were highly involved saw themselves as more skilled, successful, and satisfied. Also, parents who were more highly involved in Head Start tended to become more involved in the community after their children graduated from the program. In contrast, "where parents were not highly involved in Head Start, parents felt less able to influence their school systems and less in control of things generally." (p.20)

"The extent of parent participation is a critical variable to the benefits derived by the children from their Head Start experience." Centers with high levels of parent involvement had students with higher scores on verbal intelligence, academic achievement, self-concept, and behavior

> *Centers with high levels of parent involvement had students with higher scores on verbal intelligence, academic achievement, self-concept, and behavior in classrooms and at home.*

Parents who were more highly involved in Head Start tended to become more involved in the community after their children graduated from the program.

in classrooms and at home. The *type* of parent involvement did not appear to make a difference as much as the *extent* of parent involvement.

Findings on Program Quality and Community Change

Head Start centers with high parent involvement also fared best in program quality assessments; staff and parent chairmen reported higher quality, and evaluation teams agreed with them. These centers also reported that parents were involved in the greatest number of significant changes in community institutions

Conclusion

Centers that were high on parent involvement consistently performed better on nearly all measures of program quality, and were located in communities where significantly greater positive changes were reported in local institutions. "The study clearly indicates that extensive participation by parents in Head Start is associated with many beneficial results for children, parents, Head Start programs and communities. The best results were observed where parents were highly involved in both decision-making and learning roles." (p.61)

See also: Goodson and Hess, Gordon, Schweinhart and Weikart, Stearns and Peterson, White et al.

"The study clearly indicates that extensive participation by parents in Head Start is associated with many beneficial results for children, parents, Head Start programs and communities. The best results were observed where parents were highly involved in both decision-making and learning roles."

Nettles, Saundra Murray   EJ 436 841
"Community Involvement and Disadvantaged Students: A Review"
Review of Educational Research, Vol.61, No.3, Fall 1991, pp.379-406

SUMMARY: This review of 13 studies of community-based programs designed to improve the achievement of students at risk suggests that such efforts can have positive effects on school-related behavior and achievement as well as on attitudes and risk-taking. Nettles defines community involvement as "the actions that organizations and individuals (e.g. parents, businesses, universities, social service agencies, and the media) take to promote student development." (p.380) In the 13 studies considered, "community" refers both to locale or place, and to social interactions, which may occur outside specific boundaries.

Before looking at the data on community-based programs, Nettles suggests a typology of the change processes such programs employ:

- **Conversion**: bringing the student from one set of attitudes and behaviors to another
- **Mobilization**: increasing citizen and local-organization participation in the educational process (e.g. school-business partnerships)
- **Allocation**: providing resources such as social services or financial incentives to children and youth (e.g. the I Have a Dream program)
- **Instruction**: assisting students in their intellectual development and in learning social and civic skills.

The programs covered in this review were administered by organizations outside the formal educational system or staffed primarily by community residents or local service agencies, and were aimed mainly at students from low-income families or who were at risk of failing in school. All used at least one of the change strategies listed above; one (PUSH-EXCEL) used all four. For all 13 programs, tables list the location, main features, sampling strategy for the evaluation, measures, and level of services students received, as well as summaries of the outcomes for students.

Findings

Although the findings for programs are mixed in terms of specific outcomes (e.g. test scores, grades, attendance, continued enrollment in school, pregnancy prevention and contraceptive use, delinquency, improved attitudes, use of alcohol/tobacco), the overall direction is clear. Community-based programs "can have positive effects on school-related behaviors and achievements as well as on attitudes and risk-taking behavior. Within types of effects, the consistency of positive outcomes for attendance, pregnancy status and contraceptive behavior, and persistence in school suggests that community programs may be potentially useful interventions." (p. 397)

Community-based programs "can have positive effects on school-related behaviors and achievements as well as on attitudes and risk-taking behavior. Within types of effects, the consistency of positive outcomes for attendance, pregnancy status and contraceptive behavior, and persistence in school suggests that community programs may be potentially useful interventions."

Conclusions

Nettles offers a useful framework for examining the connections between community involvement and student progress and suggests directions for future research. "By distilling what is already known about community environments and their effects on students, by implementing ambitious action research designs in program evaluations, and by exploring connections between the various aspects of community, investigators can contribute to practical...knowledge about ways to remove impediments to the progress of disadvantaged students and can create environments that nurture those students." (p.403)

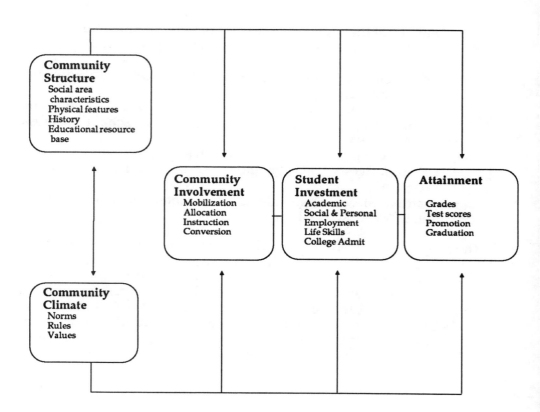

A Framework for examining community involvement and student progress

See also: Beane, Chavkin.

Olmsted, Patricia P., and Roberta I. Rubin   ED 284 839
"Linking Parent Behaviors to Child Achievement: Four Evaluation Studies
from the Parent Education Follow Through Program"
Studies in Educational Evaluation, Vol.8, 1982, pp.317-25

SUMMARY: Four intensive studies of the Parent Education Follow
Through Program find that low-income parents trained to work with
their early-elementary schoolchildren and to play other roles in the
program improved their teaching behavior at home and their
children's performance in reading and math.

Designed to help Head Start children with the transition to school, the
Parent Education Follow Through Program (PEFTP) includes parents in
the educational process, providing roles for participation ranging from
"teacher of own child" (at home) to "paid paraprofessional" (training
other parents in their homes). Home learning activities emphasize certain "Desirable Teaching Behaviors" (DTBs), aimed at inspiring a strong
relationship between parent and child. At the time of the studies, the
PEFTP was serving 4,000 elementary school children per year in eight
communities around the United States.

First, researchers verified and measured aspects of parent behavior
within program activities. Second, they assessed the relationship between these behaviors and student achievement. In three of the studies,
information about parent behavior was obtained through observation
or detailed interviews. Students' standardized test scores in reading and
math served as the measure of achievement.

Findings

Olmsted (1981) examined the use of DTBs by project parents and a
comparable group. Parents were videotaped interacting with their first-
graders on two instructional tasks. Program parents used significantly
more DTBs than the control parents.

In the second stage, a significant correlation was found between total
number of DTBs used by parents, and their children's scores for both
reading and math, providing "further evidence of a relationship between
parental teaching behavior and child school performance."

B. H. Ellis (1980) assessed the relationship between parents' frequent use
of home learning activities and student achievement in reading and
math. The experimental group included families of first-graders who
had begun the PEFTP in kindergarten; control group families had
similar ethnic and socioeconomic backgrounds but had not participated
in the program.

The first phase of this study showed that program parents used the home
activities at a very high level, while non-program families did not use
them at all. Indeed, the program parents' level of use was so high that
they had developed "a sense of...ownership in the program since they

*"As parents be-
come involved in
a variety of ways,
their own sense of
potency is en-
larged, which then
should impact
upon the child's
sense of purpose
and thus upon the
child's sense of
achievement."
--Ira Gordon,
founder of the Fol-
low Through pro-
gram*

"Home-school programs have shown that parents are not only capable, but are willing to be active participants in their children's education."

[felt] comfortable developing variations or modifications..." In the second phase, a significant relationship was found between level of use and higher reading achievement. No relationship appeared for math achievement.

B. H. Chapman (1981) examined the relationship between question-asking behavior of PEFTP parents and student achievement in reading. The investigator sorted parents' questions into seven categories, then videotaped parents of a PEFTP group and a non-program group as they read a book with their first-grade children. The videotapes were then coded for number and category of parent questions.

There was no difference in the number of questions asked by program and non-program parents; however, the PEFTP parents asked significantly more questions in five areas designated "higher level cognitive categories." In the program group, 45 percent of the improvement in child reading achievement was accounted for by the higher categories of questions asked.

Dennis Revicki (1981) studied second-grade children and their families from two PEFTP programs to investigate the relationship among factors associated with student achievement: socioeconomic status, home environment, parent involvement, and child self-concept. Parent involvement was defined as classroom volunteering in instructional and non-instructional tasks, and attendance and participation at Parent Advisory Committee meetings. He found that:

- Higher reading achievement was significantly related to the number of years of program participation, and to home visits by program staff
- Math achievement was affected only by home visits.
- Active parent involvement had a positive influence on the quantity of verbal stimulation and on parent expectations about children's educational and occupational attainment.
- Active involvement also was related to increases in student achievement and, to a lesser extent, the child's self-acceptance.

Conclusion

"Home-school programs have shown that parents are not only capable, but are willing to be active participants in their children's education." (p.11) The importance of these results lies in spreading good parental teaching behavior, beyond the DTBs in which the parents are trained. "These in-depth studies of program impact on parents and the relationship between parental behaviors and child behaviors provide valuable evidence which presents an even stronger case for the inclusion of parents as major participants in the education of their children."

See also: Bronfenbrenner, Gordon, Guinagh and Gordon, Leler, White et al.

Pfannensteil, J., T. Lambson and V. Yarnell
"Second Wave Study of the Parents as Teachers Program"
Parents as Teachers National Center, St. Louis, 1991

SUMMARY: This is a summary of evaluation findings on the Parents as Teachers Program (PAT), a parent education and support program for families with children from birth to age three. At the end of first grade, evaluators found that the PAT children scored significantly higher than comparison group children on standardized tests of reading and math, and that PAT parents were twice as likely to be involved in their children's school experiences.

PAT began in 1981, as a pilot project in four Missouri school districts. Its purpose is to strengthen the skills parents need to enhance their children's development for the first three years of life. The program has several components:

- information on child growth and development
- periodic screenings for hearing, vision, health, and general development
- monthly home visits by trained parent educators
- monthly group meetings at parent resource centers, located in neighborhood schools
- assistance in obtaining necessary social and community services.

This pilot project was first evaluated in 1985. At that time, it was determined the PAT children who had been in the program for three years showed higher achievement and language ability, and more positive social development, than comparison children, and their parents were more knowledgeable about child rearing and development. In 1989, when the PAT children completed first grade, they scored higher in reading and math, and their parents were twice as likely to be involved in their education.

In 1984, PAT was established in all Missouri school districts; two years later, an independent evaluator selected a total of 37 urban, suburban, and rural areas for a study called the "Second Wave." Within these districts, 400 families were selected by stratified sample from a group of 2500. This sample contained a higher proportion of at-risk children than is characteristic of the school population as a whole; the families were 26 percent minority, and 23 percent single-parent. Eight percent were on some form of public assistance.

Findings for Children

The performance of the children at age three was measured in terms of achievement and language ability, using the K-ABC Achievement Scale and the Preschool Language Scale.

PAT children who had been in the program for three years showed higher achievement and language ability, and more positive social development, than comparison children, and their parents were more knowledgeable about child rearing and development.

The risk areas most responsive to PAT participation are parent-child communication and developmental delays. Two-thirds of these difficulties were improved or resolved.

PAT children performed significantly higher than national norms on achievement, or about a one-half standard deviation above the norm of 100 on the K-ABC.

- More than one-half of children with observed developmental delays overcame them by age three.
- Nearly two-thirds of families with traditional characteristics of risk had children who performed at or above the national average, defying conventional expectations of low performance.

Findings for Parents/Families

- Parent knowledge about child development significantly increased for all types of families after three years' participation in the program.
- The most frequent risk for all families, difficulty in coping and family stress, was lessened or resolved for half the families within the three years.
- The risk areas most responsive to PAT participation are parent-child communication and developmental delays. Two-thirds of these difficulties were improved or resolved.
- PAT was least successful with children in families with less education, and in which English was not the primary language. (This summary did not indicate whether program information and services were available in languages other than English.)
- Parents who were eager for information and able to put it into practice were successful in supporting the social, emotional and cognitive development of their children.
- Although parents gave the entire program high ratings, they felt that the most helpful component was the home visits.

Although parents gave the entire program high ratings, they felt that the most helpful component was the home visits.

Conclusion

The study shows that when children are very young, "parents overwhelmingly prefer a parent-education and family-support program primarily based on home visits focused on the family's needs."

See also: Bronfenbrenner, Gotts, Guinagh and Gordon, Lazar, Schweinhart and Weikart, Stearns and Peterson.

Phillips, Susan D, Michael C. Smith, and John F. Witted
"Parents and Schools: Staff Report to the Study Commission on the Quality of
Education in the Metropolitan Milwaukee Schools"
Milwaukee, 1985

SUMMARY: A study of 22 school districts in the metropolitan Milwaukee area finds that parent involvement is associated with higher
school performance regardless of the income level of families served,
the grade level of the school, or the location of the school.

Eighth in a series about the Milwaukee area public schools, this report
studies the variations in parent involvement among 22 local districts. The authors cover district policies and whether they function as
intended, types of parent involvement in different schools and which
types parent organization leaders felt were most important, attitudes of
teachers, principals, and parents about parent involvement, and
whether parent involvement affects school performance.

In addition to the general data collected on student performance and
family characteristics of all schools in the districts studied, Study Commission staff conducted personal and telephone interviews with school
district superintendents and school board presidents, a mail survey of
parent organization presidents, and telephone surveys of 1594 parents
in 12 selected schools.

Findings

The findings are organized by study topics:

- **Parent involvement policies**: District policies vary considerably. Only about a third have policies with detail, another third
  have no policies at all. A model policy is included.

- **Parent organization survey**: Organizations in the suburbs have
  almost twice the number of active members as those in the
  city. Although these groups spend most of their time in fund
  raising and communications, their leaders feel they should have
  more influence on instructional activities, school policies and
  standards, and personnel decisions.

- **Teacher and principal attitudes**: Teachers report significantly
  more parent involvement at the elementary level than in high
  schools and judge that involvement to be more positive. Principals feel more positive about parent involvement than teachers,
  and feel that parents should be more active in all areas except in
  school policy and personnel.

- **Parent responses**: Parent assessment of schools is closely
  matched with actual school performance as measured by objective outcome data. Parents whose children attend higher-performing schools reported that they were much more active than

"Those schools that
do well are likely
to have active
parent organiza-
tions, numerous
volunteers, and a
high frequency of
positive interac-
tions between
parents and
teachers, but
those actions will
be backed up by
and begin with
early educational
nurturing and posi-
tive educational
expectations for
the child."

Parent assessment
of schools is closely
matched with ac-
tual school perfor-
mance as
measured by
objective
outcome data.

"The implication seems obvious. High schools should do everything possible to solicit parent involvement."

those whose children are in poorer schools. The level of reported activity was much lower at the high school level.

- **Parent involvement and school performance:** Higher-performing schools have considerably greater parent involvement, according to multiple regression analysis. Parents from higher-achieving schools reported more preschool education and higher expectations for their children.

Conclusions

"Parental involvement is generally associated with higher school performance even after we control for socio-economic background and the location of the school in the city or suburbs." (p.27) These findings also suggest that it is not just the amount of time parents spend interacting in schools or the effectiveness of that interaction that makes a difference in student achievement. Parent actions in the home and the psychological process of creating positive expectations also are likely to matter in school performance.

"Those schools that do well are likely to have active parent organizations, numerous volunteers, and a high frequency of positive interactions between parents and teachers, but those actions will be backed up by and begin with early educational nurturing and positive educational expectations for the child. Poor, uneducated single parents are less likely to be able to afford, or perhaps understand the importance of, either school or home involvement. Thus without fundamental changes, the reinforcing cycle will continue." (p.31)

See also: Coleman and Hoffer, McDill, Stevenson and Baker, Wagenaar.

Radin, Norma   EJ 067 152
"Three Degrees of Maternal Involvement in a Preschool Program: Impact on
Mothers and Children"
Child Development, December 1972, pp. 1355-1364

**SUMMARY: This study focuses on lower-IQ children in an ex-
perimental preschool program, whose mothers had counseling in
home teaching techniques. These children showed greater gains in
achievement than children whose mothers were not involved.**

The relative effects of degrees of parent involvement on children's
cognitive growth were tested in an experimental, Piaget-style preschool
program in Ypsilanti, Michigan. Three groups of children with low IQ
scores (85-98) on the Stanford-Binet test were selected.

- Group A attended 4-1/2 hours a week of preschool; their mothers
  observed bi-weekly tutorial sessions and were encouraged to
  continue the techniques at home; the mothers also attended weekly group meetings with social workers on home stimulation of
  intellectual growth.
- Group B was treated the same, except that there were no group
  meetings for the mothers.
- In Group C, the mothers were not involved at all.

Each group was tested using the Stanford-Binet and Peabody Picture
Vocabulary tests. A year after leaving the program, a pre-selected group
of children was given follow-up tests on the Wechsler Preschool and
Primary Scale of Intelligence and the Peabody Picture test.

Findings

At the end of the preschool year, all children showed significant gains
on the tests. At the end of kindergarten, only the Group A and Group B
children, whose mothers had been involved, showed continued growth
in verbal achievement. There were significant changes in the attitudes
of the mothers, "with the most change, and the most clearly desirable
changes, found in the mothers who were offered the opportunity for
maximum participation." (p.1362) The changes in the mothers appeared
to provide support for further cognitive growth in the children.

Conclusion

"...This study suggest(s) that a parent-education component is important
if the child is to continue to benefit academically from a compensatory
preschool program." (p.1363) The parent program appears to enhance
the mothers' perception of themselves as educators of their children and
of their children as individuals capable of independent thought, foster-
ing behavior that helps their children's intellectual development.

See also: Bronfenbrenner, Gotts, Lazar, Schweinhart and Weikart, White,
et al.

*"The most change,
and the most
clearly desirable
changes, were
found in the
mothers who were
offered the oppor-
tunity for
maximum
participation."*

*The changes in the
mothers appeared
to provide support
for further
cognitive growth
in the children.*

*"...a parent-educa-
tion component is
important if the
child is to continue
to benefit
academically
from a compen-
satory preschool
program."*

*Among
low-income
students,
kindergarten
readiness is critical
to future school
success.*

Reynolds, Arthur J.   ED 307 367
"A Structural Model of First-Grade Outcomes for an Urban, Low
Socioeconomical Black Population"
Paper presented at the Annual Meeting of the American Educational Research
Association, San Francisco, April 1989

SUMMARY: This study tests a model to explain the relative effects of
variables related to school readiness on the achievement of low-income, African-American first-graders. It finds that the most significant direct effect on social-emotional maturity, and one of the most
significant for reading and math achievement, is the level of parent
involvement.

Citing research finding that Black students find it more difficult than
White youngsters to recover from a difficult start in school, Reynolds
developed a model to study different influences on children's adjustment to full-time schooling. The study focuses on two general questions:

1. What are the effects (indirect and direct) of variables such as
motivation, parent involvement and mobility, on student achievement?

2. Does readiness for kindergarten have a meaningful effect on
first-grade performance?

This model is divided into three broad categories: school readiness
attributes (grade-equivalent scores on the Iowa Test of Basic Skills or
ITBS, socio-economic status, pre-kindergarten experiences); intervening
kindergarten and first-grade characteristics (e.g. motivation, parent involvement, mobility); and first-grade outcomes (reading and math ITBS
scores, and social/emotional maturity or SEMAT). The level of parent
involvement was obtained from teacher ratings on a scale of 1 to 5, from
"poor, no participation (1)" to "excellent, much participation (5)."

The model was tested on student data collected in a three-wave design,
at the beginning of kindergarten (fall 1985), at the end of kindergarten,
and again as the students completed first grade. The original sample
consisted of 1,539 children (1,470 African-Americans and 69 Hispanics)
enrolled in kindergarten classes in 26 schools serving low-income neighborhoods. Data were gathered from student records, test scores, and
teacher questionnaires.

Findings

The results of the analysis confirm that reading achievement in the first
grade is predicted by two direct variables, kindergarten readiness and
gender (in favor of girls), and two intervening variables, kindergarten
reading achievement and parent involvement in school activities. The
results for math achievement were similar, except that both prior
achievement and sex were less influential. For social/emotional
maturity (e.g. ready to learn, completes work, follows rules, works well

with others), parent involvement had the greatest direct effect, followed by sex, motivation and kindergarten math achievement.

Once the schooling process is underway, a number of variables--all possible to change--are important in first-grade achievement. One is mobility. Children who remain in the same school for both kindergarten and first grade learn more in reading and math than children who change schools. Another is motivation. And the third is parent involvement, which the author asserts can clearly be improved by teacher practices and school policies.

Conclusions

"The pervasive effects of cognitive readiness (for kindergarten), although expected, were larger than anticipated....The source of these effects derived primarily from paths through motivation, end-of-kindergarten achievement, and to a lessor extent parent involvement. These powerful effects suggest the critical importance of kindergarten readiness for future school success among low income students." (p.12)

"Parent involvement in school activities is a further influential variable that is educationally alterable....This finding is consistent with other studies and highlights the strong family-school link in the early schooling process. Of further note was that parent involvement mediated the effect of motivation on first-grade outcomes. Thus, parent involvement is also important in maintaining the effect of motivation on early school success." (p.13)

See also: Guinagh and Gordon, Mowry, Stevenson and Baker, Wong Fillmore.

"Parent involvement in school activities is a further influential variable that is educationally alterable... (and) is also important in maintaining the effect of motivation on early school success."

The most consistent predictors of children's academic achievement and social adjustment were parent expectations of their child's educational attainment and satisfaction with their child's education at school.

Reynolds, Arthur J., Nancy A. Mavrogenes, Mavis Hagemann, and Nikolaus Bezruczko
Schools, Families, and Children: Sixth Year Results from the Longitudinal Study of Children at Risk
Chicago Public Schools, Department of Research, Evaluation and Planning, February 1993

SUMMARY: This report, which presents the findings at grade six of the Longitudinal Study of Children at Risk (LSCAR), an ongoing study of low-income, minority children in the Chicago public schools, finds that parents' expectations for their children and parents' satisfaction with the school are major contributors to their children's academic and social adjustment.

Designed to explore the educational experience of children at risk, this long-term study seeks to discover the factors that contribute to their academic achievement and social adjustment. This report, completed while the children were in sixth grade, addressed three questions:

1. How well are the children doing academically and in terms of their social and emotional development?

2. What are the children's learning environments, at school, in the classroom, and at home?

3. How do the family, the school, the instruction, and their own backgrounds, particularly the aspects that can be changed, contribute to the children's adjustment?

Included in this study are 1,235 children, 95 percent are African-American, 5 percent Hispanic. Seventy percent of the families report having past or present economic hardships; only 12 percent of the children attend schools in which more than 25 percent of students score at or above the national average in reading and math.

Data were gathered from observations at school and in the classrooms, surveys and interviews of students, teacher surveys, telephone interviews with parents, standardized tests, and school records. Response frequencies and correlational analyses were used to describe the characteristics of schools, families and children, then hierarchical regression analyses identified and analyzed the factors in children's performance and adjustment.

Findings

Despite their financial hardships, the families in this study are far more diverse than the "culture of poverty" stereotype portrayed in the media. Nearly 60 percent of the parents are high school graduates, 55 percent have been married (27 percent at the time of the study), and 16 percent own their own homes. The families have lived an average of seven years at their current address. They also have positive attitudes toward their children's school and the importance of education:

- More than 90 percent like going to their child's school
- 81 percent are satisfied (49%) or very satisfied (32%) with the education their child is receiving
- 98 percent feel that school is important and 99 percent enjoy helping their children with homework
- 97 percent expect that their child will at least graduate from high school.

Furthermore, the children have positive attitudes about themselves (96 percent agree that "I am smart"), try hard in school (95%), like school (87%), and feel they get along well with others (82%). They also agree that their families support education, saying their parents ask "a lot of questions about school" (88%), make sure they do their homework (87%), and think education is very important (81%).

The most consistent predictors of children's academic achievement and social adjustment were parent expectations of their child's educational attainment and satisfaction with their child's education at school. In fact, parent satisfaction is a better predictor of achievement than is their level of involvement in the school, regardless of family background. "Community participation (organizational memberships) and...frequency of reading the newspaper also were positively associated with child outcomes, especially for achievement." (p.70)

Of the various family background variables (e.g. education level, income), the only one that contributed above and beyond family process variables (e.g. read to child, help with homework) was home ownership. The researchers conclude that children's adjustment and achievement "is due not just to differences in family background such as low income, but to parents' expectations and attitudes as well as to how they spend their time." (p.71)

Conclusions

The authors found it surprising that parents generally gave positive ratings to their children's education at school, when the overwhelming majority of schools have very low achievement (75 percent of children scoring below the national average). They suggest three reasons for this discrepancy: parents may feel that other schools are even worse, that closeness to home and good relations with teachers are more important than academics, or they may be too easily satisfied. Because parent satisfaction is associated with higher student achievement, the authors feel "this finding emphasizes the importance of aligning the interests of families and schools in educational improvement efforts and reinforces this priority to school reform efforts." (p.78)

See also: Dauber and Epstein, Epstein, Melnick and Fiene

"Community participation (organizational memberships) and...frequency of reading the newspaper also were positively associated with child outcomes, especially for achievement."

Despite their financial hardships, the families in this study are far more diverse than the "culture of poverty" stereotype portrayed in the media.

- *60% are high school graduates*
- *55% have been married*
- *16% own their own homes.*
- *They have lived an average of 7 years at current address, and they have positive attitudes toward school.*

"Dropouts, in
general have
lower grades,
poorer atten-
dance records,
and more and
severer disciplinary
problems than do
other students."

Rumberger, Russell W., Rita Ghatak, Gary Poulos, Philip L. Ritter, and Sanford
M. Dornbusch
"Family Influences on Dropout Behavior in One California High School"
Sociology of Education, Vol.63, October, 1990, pp.283-299

SUMMARY: Examining family processes and how they influence high
school student achievement and dropout behavior, this study finds
that dropouts are more likely to come from families in which parents
are less involved in their children's education.

In recent years, researchers have devoted much effort to understanding
why students drop out before completing high school. Although they
have identified demographic, family-related, school-related, and individual factors, these do not explain the underlying processes that
actually lead to dropout behavior. This article examines how families
behave and interact, or "family process variables," to determine if they
also play a role in influencing students' decisions to drop out of school.

Reviewing the research on student achievement, the authors suggest
several ways in which families, through their attitudes and behavior,
influence their children's performance in school:

- Parents become involved with teachers and schools
- Parents spend time with their children, pursuing educational
  activities
- Parents impart values, aspirations, and motivation needed to
  persevere in school
- Parenting styles promote good communication and responsible
  behavior.

Much of the data used came from recent surveys of students and parents
that the researchers conducted in six San Francisco high schools. For the
present study, 114 students who dropped out of school in the 1985-86
school year were identified. Of these, 48 had previously completed the
surveys mentioned above. These were matched by sex, ethnicity, grade
level, and family structure to a control group of 48 students still attending school.

The variables examined to determine their relationship to dropout
behavior were:

1. Family decision-making practices: especially whether the student
or the parents make the important decisions (e.g. choosing clothes,
how late to stay out)

2. Parenting style: whether authoritative, permissive, or
authoritarian, following the typology used in the authors' other
studies

3. Parent reactions to grades: whether students were punished or
encouraged, or parents had negative emotions about bad grades

4. Parents' educational involvement: including attendance at school events and helping children with homework

5. Students' educational involvement: including paying attention, cutting classes, and doing homework.

Other variables in the study were television viewing practices, whether the student had a quiet place to study, educational aspirations and expectations, and number of hours students were employed per week.

Findings

In terms of ethnicity, gender, grade level and family structure, dropouts do not differ significantly from students who stay in school. There are, however, sharp contrasts in grades, attendance, and behavioral problems; "dropouts, in general have lower grades, poorer attendance records, and more and severer disciplinary problems than do other students." (p.292) The analysis also reveals some important differences in the family process variables. All five factors listed above were associated with the student's decision to stay in school or drop out. Students who drop out report:

- Fewer decisions made jointly with parents and more decisions made individually
- Households characterized by a permissive parenting style
- Parents who are more likely to use punishments and to react to poor grades with negative emotions
- Parents who are much less involved in their education
- Less involvement in their own education when they were in school, spending less time on homework, cutting class, and paying less attention when they did attend school.

Conclusion

"The strongest pattern that emerges...is the lower level of educational involvement exhibited by dropouts and their parents compared to other students." (p.295) Parent involvement includes monitoring and helping students with homework, attending school conferences and functions, and providing a supportive learning environment at home. Because they do poorly in school, dropouts probably need more assistance than other students, yet they report lower levels of parental involvement.

The authors conclude that strategies to assist at-risk students should "attempt to strengthen parental involvement so that both schools and families can provide the support and assistance students need to succeed in school. It is not true that parents are unable or unwilling to change their parenting of adolescents; they can and do change their approaches and expectations." (p.297)

See also: Clark (1983), Dornbusch, Snow et al., Steinberg et al., Stevenson and Baker

"What most distinguishes dropouts from other low-achieving students who stay in school is the lower levels of educational involvement exhibited by dropouts and their parents compared to other students."

Sattes, Beth D.
"Parent Involvement: A Review of the Literature"
Occasional Paper #021, Appalachia Educational Laboratory, 1031 Quarrier St.,
Charleston, WV, 25325, November 1985

SUMMARY: Reviewing studies of home and family influences on student achievement at all grade levels, the author finds that parent attitudes most associated with high achievement can be positively shaped by involvement with schools, and can also contribute to improving attendance, motivation, self-concept and positive behavior. All that is required is administrative commitment, staff training, and a variety of options for parents.

After reviewing over thirty studies on the connection between family background and school achievement, Sattes suggests that while certain fixed characteristics such as family size and socioeconomic status (SES) are associated with higher achievement, other more complex variables, which *are* subject to change, are also related to high performance. Reading to children, having books available, taking trips, guiding TV watching, and providing stimulating experiences all contribute to school achievement. "The fact that family SES is related to school achievement doesn't mean that rich kids are born smarter. It means that, in more affluent families, children are more likely to be exposed to experiences that stimulate intellectual development." (p.2)

Findings for Preschool

Early childhood programs such as Head Start, which help children become ready for school, have improved children's achievement, especially in the early grades. Yet if parents are not involved in these programs, the benefits rarely persist into the long-term. "Parent involvement is the key to long-lasting effects from preschool programs. Evidently a change occurs in the home environment which supports and maintains school achievement." (p. 5)

Findings for Kindergarten to High School

Although the results of preschool programs are widely documented, parent involvement also has positive effects on student achievement during the years in school:

- **Improved academic performance:** When parents are trained as tutors, children gain in both reading and math, although this approach appears to be most effective through third grade. Benefits also appear when parents support and encourage their children's learning, such as reading and talking to them about school, and when parents praise and reward good performance.

- **Improved student attendance:** If schools contact parents when their children are absent, either by telephone or notes, attendance improves.

One junior high school class whose parents had individual meetings with counselors the summer before seventh grade not only had higher attendance rates, but also better grades and lower dropout rates, compared to the class entering the year before.

- Improved motivation: Most studies that measure the effects of parent involvement on student attitudes toward learning report a significant and positive effect.

- **Increased self-esteem:** When parents are part of a school's intervention to help children feel better about themselves, children's self-concept improves. A program to increase parents' academic expectations for their children resulted in both improved student self-esteem and higher grades.
- **Improved student behavior:** Home-based reinforcement systems, in which teachers regularly inform parents of behavior in school, result in more appropriate conduct, especially when parents reward good behavior.

What Does It Take?

"For a school to have an effective parent-involvement program, administrators, teachers, and parents must believe that parent involvement is important and be willing to work together." (p.17) But meaningful involvement is not commonplace; it requires:

1. **Commitment from administrators:**
   - Formal, written policies
   - Direction and guidance for parents
   - Clear and high expectations that parent involvement is a key to improved schools

2. **Training:**
   - In-service training for teachers
   - Staff involvement in planning and evaluating the parent program
   - Opportunities for parents to learn the skills and knowledge to be good partners

3. **A variety of options for parents:**
   - Appropriate opportunities, depending on age and grade level of child, and family circumstances
   - School-wide communication system at the secondary level.

Conclusions

Although benefits are documented for parent involvement at all age levels, "the evidence presents a powerful argument for home-based or parent-involved preschool programs for all children, because never again in a child's career can a program result in such permanent and significant positive effects." (p.22) Nevertheless, Sattes recommends as a "worthwhile investment" parent involvement programs at all levels that take into account changes in the parent-child, teacher-child and peer group relationships as children progress through school.

See also: Becher, Kellaghan, Leler, Ziegler.

"The evidence presents a powerful argument for home-based or parent-involved preschool programs for all children, because never again in a child's career can a program result in such permanent and significant positive effects."

"The fact that family SES is related to school achievement doesn't mean that rich kids are born smarter. It means that, in more affluent families, children are more likely to be exposed to experiences that stimulate intellectual development."

> The expectations of parents and their own level of attainment has a primary influence on their children's goals and whether they are able to attain them.

> For girls, only ten percent who aspired to a high-level occupation actually attained it; the higher their mothers' educational level, the more likely they were to succeed.

Schiamberg, Lawrence B. and Cong-Hee Chun
"The Influence of Family on Educational and Occupational Achievement"
Department of Family and Child Ecology, Michigan State University
Paper presented at the American Association for the Advancement of Science
Annual Meeting, Philadelphia, 1986

SUMMARY: **A fourteen-year longitudinal study of rural, low-income youth finds that the family makes significant contributions to the attainment of educational and occupational goals.**

In 1969, 1202 students attending fifth and sixth grades in rural, low-income areas in six southeastern states were surveyed, along with their mothers. In 1975, 1978, and 1983, subsamples of the original group were re-interviewed, as high school students, young adults, and as adults. Using a causal/path model technique to assess the relative effects of various important influences on educational and occupational attainment, the authors looked at family background, characteristics of the students (mental ability, self-concept, academic motivation), achievement motivation, and family members and significant others.

Findings

The authors found three major predictors of educational attainment: (1) The youth's aspirations, (2) The child's characteristics, and (3) Parent influence.

The total effect of family influence on students' ability to attain their occupational goals was greater than the effects of both the students' characteristics and their educational attainment. The influence of family on educational attainment was even more significant. The expectations of parents and their own level of attainment has a primary influence on their children's goals and whether they are able to attain them.

The more confidence a high school male had that he would achieve his desired occupation, the more likely he was to attain it as a young adult. For girls, only ten percent who aspired to a high-level occupation actually attained it; the higher their mothers' educational level, the more likely they were to succeed.

Conclusion

The effect of family background on educational attainment is significant both directly and indirectly. "Although its direct associations of family background factors with youth's educational attainment is not one of the strongest, the total effects mediated through such variables as child's characteristics, significant other's influence, and achievement motivation, were found to be strongest of all the independent variables tested in this study." (p.31)

See also: Baker and Stevenson, Clark (1983), Eagle.

Schweinhart, Lawrence J. and David P. Weikart
"The High/Scope Perry Preschool Study, Similar Studies, and Their Implications for Public Policy in the U.S."
In Early Childhood Education: Policy Issues for the 1990's, *Stegelin, Dolores A., ed., Norwood, NJ: Ablex Publishing Corporation, 1992*

SUMMARY: This paper reviews studies of high-quality preschool programs that work with families, and finds significant social, academic, and economic benefits over the long-term for students. The authors estimate that a national investment in quality childcare programs for all children would yield a net return of $31.6 billion each year, from reduced costs for social services and criminal justice, and from increases in productivity and tax revenues.

While many studies have documented positive effects of preschool programs for children of low-income and working mothers, the social and economic implications of making such programs universally available have not been calculated in concise detail. In this paper, the authors examine the findings of the High/Scope Perry Preschool study and other longitudinal studies of programs serving young children living in poverty and at risk of school failure.

The High/Scope Perry Preschool Study

This study followed 123 people who lived in the attendance area of the Perry Elementary School in Ypsilanti, Michigan, for 25 years. In 1962, all were four-years-old or younger, in poverty, with low intelligence-test scores. Half the group was randomly assigned to the Perry Preschool; the other half received no preschool program.

The Perry program developed the High/Scope curriculum, which promotes intellectual, social and physical development, and allows children to initiate their own learning activities, with support from teachers. All teachers were certified in special education and early-childhood education and taught no more than six children. Class sessions lasted 2-1/2 hours, once or twice a week, for 30 weeks a year. The children attended for two years. Parents were treated as partners in the process. Once a week, a teacher visited each family at home for 1-1/2 hours to discuss the child's progress and to model parent-child activities.

Sources of data for the long-term study include:
- Parent interviews (when children were at ages 3 and 15)
- Annual intelligence and language tests (at ages 3-10; and 14)
- Annual achievement tests (at ages 7-11; and at 14 and 19)
- Participant interviews (at ages 15, 19, and 28)
- School record information (at ages 11, 15, and 19)
- Police and social services records (at ages 19 and 28)

"Because of this intellectual boost, the preschool group achieved greater school success than the no-preschool group--higher school achievement and literacy, better placement in school, stronger commitment to schooling, and more years of school completed."

"Early childhood education seems to produce its long-term effects not through sustained improvements in intelligence, as was once hoped, but by equipping children to be more successful students...their success breeds higher motivation, better performance, and higher regard from teachers and classmates."

Findings

The results are striking. The preschool group surpassed the no-preschool group in intellectual performance consistently from ages four to seven. "Because of this intellectual boost, the preschool group achieved greater school success than the no-preschool group--higher school achievement and literacy, better placement in school, stronger commitment to schooling, and more years of school completed." This success in school probably contributed to the greater economic success and social responsibility of the preschool group during the teenage years.

Outcome	Age Measured	Preschool	No Preschool
Years in Special Education	19	16%	28%
Do Homework	15	68%	40%
High School Graduates	19	67%	49%
Employed	19	50%	32%
On Welfare	19	18%	32%
Ever Arrested	19	31%	51%

Conclusions

"Early childhood education seems to produce its long-term effects not through sustained improvements in intelligence, as was once hoped, but by equipping children to be more successful students...their success breeds higher motivation, better performance, and higher regard from teachers and classmates." (p.77)

Low-quality early-childhood programs do not produce the kinds of long-term benefits documented in these studies; they may even have negative effects. Effective programs share these characteristics:

- Explicit, developmentally appropriate curricula that support children's self-initiated learning activities
- Trained teaching staff with low staff turnover
- In-service training and supervisory support for staff
- Two adult teachers for every 20 children ages three to five
- Home visits or other forms of intensive parent involvement.

"Although the costs of good early-childhood programs for the nation are great, the eventual costs of not providing them, in money and in decreased quality of life, are greater."

The authors calculate that extending such programs to all children in need would save taxpayers $31.6 billion a year from reduced costs for special education, injuries to crime victims, criminal penalties, and welfare benefits. "Although the costs of good early-childhood programs for the nation are great, the eventual costs of not providing them, in money and in decreased quality of life, are greater." (p.83)

See also: Bronfenbrenner, Guinagh and Gordon, Gotts, Lazar, Mowry, Radin, Reynolds.

Scott-Jones, Diane
"Family Influences on Cognitive Development and School Achievement" In
Review of Research in Education, *Vol.11, 1984, Chap.7, pp. 259-304*

SUMMARY: This review discusses the research on ways that families
influence children's cognitive development and school achievement,
including biological and environmental factors, as well as family
processes such as parent-child interaction and parents' aspirations
and expectations for the child's educational achievement.

Scott-Jones begins by examining the assumptions underlying the research on the relationship of family influences to cognitive development.
Researchers generally concur that:

1. A child's knowledge and understanding grow, in part, from
interactions with other people
2. The entire family system (including fathers and siblings) is important
3. The influences are two-way; a child's behavior and attitudes may
influence the parents as well as the reverse
4. Parent-child interactions occur within the broader society and
culture.

Findings on Family Background

The biological factors considered are: genetic influences, health, and
nutrition. Lack of adequate nutrition during pregnancy and the child's
infancy may have a negative effect on intellectual development. The
impact of low birth weight can be lessened, however, by giving children
extra stimulation and helping mothers to provide nurturing environments.

Environmental factors include the physical setting, such as extreme lack
of stimulation or an excess of crowding and noise in the home. Having
some personal space and relief from noise appears to improve children's
performance in school.

Status variables that are influential in the child's cognitive development
and achievement are: family configuration, single-parent families, the
employment of the mother outside the home, socioeconomic status, and
race or ethnicity. The author provides a thorough discussion of the
effects of single-parent households and the mother's daily absence from
the home if she enters the work force. Scott-Jones stresses that it is
important for educators and researchers not to emphasize the deficiencies that may result from these changes in family structure and status,
but instead to focus on the ways in which any and all family members
can cope with adverse conditions.

Findings on Family Processes

Studies on family processes address such topics as the parents' style of
interaction with the child, strategies for teaching the child at home, and
how parents' beliefs and expectations can affect student achievement.

*It is important for educators and re-
searchers not to
emphasize the
deficiencies that
may result from
these changes in
family structure
and status, but in-
stead to focus on
the ways in which
any and all family
members can
cope with adverse
conditions.*

*"Teachers need to
be sensitive to the
needs of children
from various family
backgrounds, such
as single-parent
families or families
with working
parents, and must
also be careful to
avoid stereotyped
expectations of
children from
various back-
grounds."*

"There is a strong positive relationship between the accuracy of parents' achievement expectations and children's performance on cognitive tasks. It appears important that parents hold...expectations that are relatively close to children's current performance level."

Scott-Jones makes an important distinction between aspirations and expectations: researchers have documented that lower-class parents have high aspirations for their children's future educational achievement but they also demonstrate lower expectations for academic performance in the short run. This results in a value "stretch," referring to the greater distance between aspirations and expectations in lower-class families than is the case in middle-class families.

Scott-Jones also suggests a model for understanding the relationship between expectations and performance. Parents' expectations and aspirations are communicated to the child; the child perceives and uses them to develop self-expectation, which ultimately affects academic performance. "There is a strong positive relationship between the accuracy of parents' achievement expectations and children's performance on cognitive tasks. It appears important that parents hold...expectations that are relatively close to children's current performance level." (p.292)

Conclusion

The author concludes that "Many facets of family experience interact to influence the child's cognitive development....Although a general increase in the standard of living of the poor may be required for major change to occur, the strategy that has been used more widely is to encourage parents to participate more actively in their children's education." (p. 294)

See also: Kellaghan et al., Milne, Stevenson and Baker, Ziegler.

Scott-Jones, Diane
*"Mother-As-Teacher in the Families of High- and Low-Achieving Low-Income
Black First-Graders"*
Journal of Negro Education, *Vol.56, No.1, 1987, pp.21-34*

SUMMARY: This exploratory study finds significant differences in
how low-income Black mothers of high- and low-achieving first-
graders approach teaching their children. Mothers of high achievers
tend to have clear goals for their children's education, play a supportive and less formal role, and let their children initiate learning
activities.

The sample for this study consisted of 24 Black first-graders, from
low-income families living in a small, southern university town during
the 1978-79 school year. Scores on the Metropolitan Readiness Test were
used to select 16 "low-readiness" (2nd-12th percentile) and eight "high-
readiness" (51st-88th percentile) children.

Data on the families were gathered from the following sources:

- **Naturalistic observations:** Interactions between the children and
  their families at home were observed, during two 40-minute
  sessions about one week apart. Behaviors of mothers and children
  were coded, in categories including teaching, talking about
  school, praise for school-related activity, play, and TV watching.

- **Maternal teaching task:** Mothers were taught Parcheesi, then
  asked to teach it to their child. The behaviors of the mother and
  child during learning and playing were coded.

- **Interviews:** Mothers were interviewed about the family's income
  and education, routines, child-rearing practices, and values and
  attitudes related to education.

- **School records:** Information on the children's performance and
  behavior were taken from California Achievement Test scores,
  teacher assessments, and attendance.

Findings

Although many behaviors were the same in both high- and low- achieving children's families, there were a few significant differences:

1. **Goals and expectations:** Mothers in high-readiness families expressed clear academic goals for their children and strongly communicated the value of education. Mothers of low-readiness
children voiced high aspirations for their children in the future, but
had lower expectations for day-to-day success.

2. **Teaching methods:** High-readiness children tended to initiate
educational activities, while the mothers played an informal, sup-

*Mothers of low-
readiness children
voiced high aspira-
tions for their
children in the fu-
ture, but had
lower expecta-
tions for day-to-
day success.*

*"High-readiness
children appeared
to take the lead in
their own activities,
and mothers
responded when
needed. In high-
readiness homes,
teaching and
school-related ac-
tivities were in-
tegrated into the
flow of pleasant
play activities, and
were not formal
and intentional."*

In one high-readiness family, the child played "store" with her cousin, using dolls, play money, and stuffed toys. The mother watched them, making suggestions and comments, helping when necessary, and laughing at the children's funny remarks.

portive role. Low-readiness mothers were more formal and intentional, and their style was rigid and academic, possibly because of insecurity about their ability.

3.**Educational background:** All but one of the high-readiness mothers, but only half the low-readiness mothers, had completed high school. Although all 24 families had approximately the same income, about one-third of the low-readiness families, but none of the high-readiness families, were receiving public assistance.

4.**Values and practices related to education:** High-readiness families had more books at home and higher goals for the child in high school and as an adult. For example, all the high-readiness mothers mentioned being smart and getting good grades, while the low-readiness mothers more often mentioned good behavior.

5. **Children's behavior:** High-readiness children were more likely to take the initiative in home learning activities, asking questions and taking the lead in playing the game. The low-readiness children took a more passive role; the mothers had to motivate their children to read or play the game, as well as provide directions and explanations.

Conclusions

Mothers of children who are well prepared for first grade are supportive, responding to children's requests for attention rather than directing their activities. "High-readiness children appeared to take the lead in their own activities, and mothers responded when needed. In high-readiness homes, teaching and school-related activities were integrated into the flow of pleasant play activities, and were not formal and intentional." (p.33)

The fact that mothers of children not as ready for first grade take a more formal, teacher-like approach with their children raises a caution. "The current popular educational practice of encouraging parental help with children's schoolwork needs to be carefully implemented and needs to be informed by more extensive research." (p.34)

See also: Clark (1993), Leler, Olmsted and Rubin, Reynolds.

Simich-Dudgeon, Carmen
"Increasing Student Achievement Through Teacher Knowledge About Parent Involvement"
In Families and Schools in a Pluralistic Society, Chavkin, Nancy Feyl, ed., (Albany: State University of New York Press, 1993), Chapter 10, pp.189-204

SUMMARY: After discussing characteristics of successful programs to involve parents who speak little or no English, the author reports on a multi-cultural project in two high schools where staff were trained to work with limited-English families, and parents were trained to use home-learning lessons with their children. Students made significant gains in English comprehension, fluency, vocabulary, grammar, and pronunciation.

Efforts to involve parents with limited English skills have not been seriously encouraged in the public schools. Simich-Dudgeon argues that there is "an urgent need" to train teachers and key administrators in cross-cultural skills and in how to initiate and maintain communication with parents who have limited English proficiency (LEP).

Many parents from the Hispanic and Asian cultures believe that teachers and administrators are the professional experts; to contact the school shows disrespect or interference. In addition, parents who do not speak English may feel they cannot help their children.

Rather than replacing these attitudes with ones that conform to American culture, Simich-Dudgeon suggests that school staff use "an additive model of parent acculturation." This approach recognizes and appreciates the family's culture, then seeks to add new roles for the parents to play at home and in the school.

Simich-Dudgeon suggests that school staff use "an additive model of parent acculturation." This approach recognizes and appreciates the family's culture, then seeks to add new roles for the parents to play at home and in the school.

The Trinity-Arlington Project

From 1983 to 1986, this program trained parents from four language groups (Spanish, Vietnamese, Khmer, and Lao) in home tutoring strategies. Although the project was implemented at all three levels of schooling, this report discusses the experience at the two high schools, where the families of 350 students participated. Eighty percent of the parents spoke little or no English.

The project had three components: teacher training in techniques for involving parents, parent training, and curriculum development. During the training, school staff developed 19 home-learning lessons, called Vocationally Oriented Bilingual Curriculum (VOBC), designed to bring parent and child together as co-learners, on such topics as "You and Your Guidance Counselor" and "Career Planning."

Findings

The project evaluation showed that students made significant gains from pre-test to post-test on all measures of the SOLOM English oral language proficiency test (comprehension, fluency, vocabulary, grammar, and pronunciation) as well as in writing. In addition, the frequency and type of parent contacts with schools increased, and parents reported that they knew more about the school system.

"More important, students reported that they discussed the home lessons not only with the parent or guardian but also with siblings and other extended-family members. This finding raises interesting possibilities about sibling cooperative learning at home when parents or guardians are not available to participate....It also suggests that parental involvement must be seen as including (or potentially including) other family members." (p.198)

Conclusions

Features of Successful Parent Involvement Programs

The following preconditions help to maintain effective programs:

- Coordinating LEP parent involvement efforts at the school district level, including hiring parent coordinators and community liaisons
- Setting up a two-way communication system at each school, for all language groups
- Providing information on local health and community services
- Planning the program within a framework of several years
- Developing LEP family profiles to understand the structure and circumstances of the families to be involved.

In addition to these supports, successful programs share certain key features:

1. **Clear and focused goals:** If the program focuses on training parents to tutor their children at home, for example, teachers should choose a few selected skills to teach the parents

2. **Simple, easy to implement, but highly motivational materials:** Materials and directions should be fully explained to the parents, and followed up frequently

3. **Ongoing monitoring and assessment:** Parents and students should be surveyed about their reactions to the activities, communications, and their effects; teachers should keep a record of their efforts

4. **Developing parent-as-tutor skills:** Parents should be trained in techniques for verbal interaction that promote cognitive and language development (recalling facts, comparing things, defending a point of view, explaining conclusions reached).

See also: Becher, Comer, Goldenburg, Leler, Wong Fillmore.

"More important, students reported that they discussed the home lessons not only with the parent or guardian but also with siblings and other extended-family members. This finding raises interesting possibilities about sibling cooperative learning at home when parents or guardians are not available to participate."

Snow, Catherine E., Wendy S. Barnes, Jean Chandler, Irene F. Goodman, and
Lowry Hemphill
Unfulfilled Expectations: Home and School Influences on Literacy,
(Cambridge: Harvard University Press, 1991)

SUMMARY: This book describes a study of home and school influences on literacy achievement among children from low-income families, which found that the single variable most positively connected to all literacy skills was formal parent-school involvement.

Noting that "studies of failure in literacy achievement have tended to shift the blame back and forth between home and school, in cycles of about 20 years," the authors conclude that factors at both home and school are responsible for success in literacy.

The researchers studied 32 low-income children in grades two, four, and six, attending five elementary schools in a small industrial city in the Northeast. About half the children selected were performing somewhat above average; the remainder were just below. Although all families were English-speaking, the sample was varied in terms of family size and structure, mother's education level, parents' employment status, and family income. The children and their families were studied for two school years, from 1980-1982.

Data were collected from school records, interviews with children, parents, teachers, and siblings, and from observations in the classrooms and the homes. Student achievement was measured in tests of four literacy skills: word recognition, vocabulary, writing, and reading comprehension.

Findings

To organize their observations, the researchers proposed three models of how families affect children's literacy and language achievement.

"Family as Educator" looks at the parent's role in helping with homework, the literacy environment of the home, and parent expectations for the child's educational achievement. The educational role parents play at home had a significant, positive effect on children's word recognition and vocabulary.

"Resilient Family" describes a supportive home environment in which "children develop self-confidence and a positive self-image, have positive expectations about their relations with teachers and other adults, have experienced success after persistence at difficult tasks, and can set goals and regulate their own behavior."(p.91) The literacy skill most strongly related to the resilient family is children's writing.

"Parent-School Partnership" examines formal parent-school involvement, contacts with teachers, homework help, parent-child interaction about education, and school attendance. Of these, the one most sig-

The steep drop in students' prospects and performance once they entered secondary school appears to be directly related to the decline in the supports the researchers identified as key to achievement: formal contacts between home and school, out-of-school literacy experiences, and cooperative relationships with teachers.

Contacts between teachers and parents also brought positive results, such as more positive teacher assessment of the family, parent communication with the school, improved schoolwork, and gains on reading achievement tests.

nificantly correlated with all four literacy outcomes was formal parent-school involvement. This included active PTA participation, attending school activities, and serving as a volunteer. No other variable in the study had such a strong effect on all four literacy skills.

The researchers hypothesize three reasons for the effectiveness of formal parental involvement:

- it provided parents with information about the school environment so they could better prepare their children
- it demonstrated to children that school was important
- it enhanced children's potential in their teachers' eyes, thus providing extra help and raised expectations.

Contacts between teachers and parents also brought positive results, such as more positive teacher assessment of the family, parent communication with the school, improved schoolwork, and gains on reading achievement tests. The families were in turn more likely to initiate subsequent contacts, and teachers believed that such contacts contributed to the child's success in school.

"If no personal contact existed between home and school, the teachers tended to assume the worst about parental willingness and ability to contribute to their children's education." (p. 139)

Conclusions

The authors conclude this book with a sobering epilogue, describing a follow-up study on 28 of the children when they were in seventh, ninth, and eleventh grades. Nearly all the older children had serious difficulty adjusting to high school, and few reported having close or supportive relations with teachers or adults outside their family. "Few of the students in the study had continued to make gains in literacy consonant with their abilities. Only a small minority were taking courses that would qualify them for entry to college. Several were high school dropouts, and very few planned to go on to training of any sort after high school." (p.213)

This steep drop in students' prospects and performance once they entered secondary school appears to be directly related to the decline in the supports the researchers identified as key to achievement: formal contacts between home and school, out-of-school literacy experiences, and cooperative relationships with teachers. Parents became intimidated by the array of high school staff--assistant principals, guidance counselors, department chairs--and tended to have no contact with school personnel once their children left junior high.

See also: Baker and Stevenson, Lareau, Schiamberg and Chun, Wong Fillmore.

Stearns, Mariam Sherman and Susan Peterson, et. al.   *ED 088 588*
"Parent Involvement in Compensatory Education Programs: Definitions and Findings"
Menlo Park Educational Policy Research Center, Stanford Research Institute, Stanford, August 1973

SUMMARY: This major review of federal evaluation reports suggests that there is a connection between parent involvement and institutional change and that involving parents as tutors and trainers can have positive effects on children's IQ scores.

This is the first major review of evaluation data on federal compensatory education programs that attempted to relate parent involvement to student achievement. At that early date in the history of these programs, there was rather little data showing measurable improvement in children's achievement from compensatory education programs. The authors, therefore, found it difficult to correlate any features of the programs with success, much less to pinpoint parent involvement. It is a very thoughtful analysis, nevertheless, and explores a number of important issues.

Findings

In these programs, there are three major roles for parents to play: tutors, employees, and decision-makers. There is evidence that involving parents as trainers and tutors can improve children's performance, especially that of young, preschool children. The effects vary directly with the intensity and length of the program and appear in both the children's IQ scores and in parents' attitudes about themselves.

The findings on the effect of employing parents as classroom aides or community workers are sparse, largely because programs that do so also introduce many other changes into the classroom. In preschool projects staffed primarily by paraprofessionals, "positive impacts on participating children have been demonstrated."

The effects of parent involvement in decision making on children's academic performance are particularly difficult to measure and evaluate, because they cannot be easily isolated from other factors and because they take longer to show up.

The authors speculate that parent involvement affects achievement because the different roles parents play set certain chains of events in motion. When parents learn to teach their own children, they not only give their children new skills but also build their own feelings of competence. This in turn motivates the children to perform better, setting a cycle of success-reinforcement in motion. (See chart on next page.)

When parents learn to teach their own children, they not only give their children new skills but also build their own feelings of competence. This in turn motivates the children to perform better, setting a cycle of success-reinforcement in motion.

For parent involvement to be effective, it must be carefully organized, with clear guidelines for substantive participation.

Conclusion

Stearns et al. conclude that for parent involvement to be effective, it must be carefully organized, with clear guidelines for substantive participation.

Positive Reinforcement Cycle from Parent Involvement

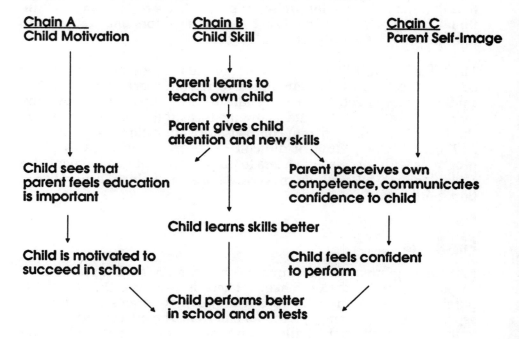

See also: Goodson and Hess, Gordon, Lazar, Pfannensteil.

Steinberg, Laurence, Nina S. Mounts, Susie D. Lamborn, and Sanford Dornbusch   ED 324 558
"Authoritative Parenting and Adolescent Adjustment Across Varied Ecological Niches"
Based on a paper presented at the biennial meeting of the Society for Research in Child Development, Kansas City, MO, April 1989

SUMMARY: This study examines the relationship between "authoritative parenting" and achievement among 8,000 high school students. Regardless of ethnicity, social class, or family structure, adolescents whose parents are accepting, firm, and democratic earn higher grades in school, are more self-reliant, report less anxiety and depression, and are less likely to engage in delinquent behavior.

Previous research on parenting styles has shown a strong correlation between authoritative parenting practices and high achievement in school for middle-class Anglo-American students, but not necessarily for students from other social and ethnic backgrounds. This study attempts to determine if authoritative parenting practices result in higher achievement among low-income and minority families.

The sample for the study was comprised of 8,000 students enrolled in grades 9-12 at nine high schools in Wisconsin and California. The schools were selected to yield a diverse ethnic sample: nine percent Black, 14 percent Asian-American, 12 percent Hispanic, and 60 percent Anglo-American. The students responded to two self-report questionnaires.

The three characteristics of an authoritative parenting style are:

   1. **Acceptance and Involvement:** The extent to which the adolescent sees his parents as loving and responsive
   2. **Firm Control:** The degree of parent monitoring and setting of limits
   3. **Psychological Autonomy:** The use of noncoercive, democratic discipline, and encouragement to express individuality within the family.

Three demographic variables were collected for each student: socioeconomic status (middle class or working class), family structure (intact two-parent family or not), and ethnicity (Anglo-American, Hispanic-American, African-American, and Asian-American).

The four dependent variables, or outcomes for students, were:

   1. Grade point average
   2. Self-reliance, on the Psycho-Social Maturity Inventory
   3. Psychological distress, from the Center for Epidemiologic Studies Depression Scale (e.g. anxiety, insomnia, fatigue)
   4. Delinquency, according to self-reported involvement in delinquent activities.

Authoritative families have these qualities:

*1. **Acceptance and Involvement:** Students say, "I can count on my parents to help me out if I have a problem."*

*2. **Firm Control:** Students say, "My parents try to know where I go at night".*

*3. **Psychological Autonomy:** Students say: "My parents do not tell me that their ideas are correct and that I should not question them."*

Sixteen data cells were formed on the basis of the four ethnic groups, two socioeconomic status categories, and two family structures. The four adolescent adjustment variables were then calculated for each of the 16 cells, creating a total of 64 "ecological niches."

Findings

Of the 64 ecological groups, 40 showed statistically significant results, demonstrating that students from authoritative families show positive results for all four outcomes: higher grades, more self-reliance, less psychological distress, and less delinquent activity. This pattern was more common among middle-class families than working-class, among Anglo-American families than minority families, and among intact than non-intact families.

Because the number of cases in some of the 64 cells was low, further analysis tried to determine whether authoritative practices yielded positive results for certain subgroups, e.g. African-American working-class families or Asian-American middle-class families. The results show that three of the outcomes--self-reliance, lack of psychological distress, and less delinquency--were related to authoritative parenting practices, but grade-point average was not affected. The relationship between authoritative parenting and school performance was greater among Anglo-American and Hispanic-American adolescents than among African-Americans or Asian-Americans, confirming the findings of earlier studies.

The researchers discuss the limitations of the study's design and methodology, which make it impossible to be certain that the parenting practices identified have caused or even preceded the outcomes. Only longitudinal studies can establish a clear linkage. Another limitation is the reliance on self-reported information, rather than on outside observation. In this study, using questionnaires allowed the researchers to use a much larger sample than would be feasible for a design requiring observation.

"The results of the present study provide evidence that ... virtually regardless of their family background, adolescents whose parents are warm, firm, and democratic enjoy psychological and behavioral advantages over their peers."

Conclusion

"The results of the present study provide evidence that the...positive correlation between parental authoritativeness and adolescent adjustment appears to transcend ethnicity, socioeconomic status, and family structure. Virtually regardless of their family background, adolescents whose parents are warm, firm, and democratic enjoy psychological and behavioral advantages over their peers." (pp.15-16)

See also: Clark (1983), Dornbusch, Eagle.

Stevenson, David L. and David P. Baker   *EJ 362 736*
"The Family-School Relation and the Child's School Performance,"
Child Development, *Vol.58, 1987, pp.1348-1357*

SUMMARY: This study finds that children's school performance is positively related to parent involvement in school activities, regardless of the mother's educational background or the child's age. Parents of girls tend to stay more involved and have more influence on achievement than parents of boys.

Research on the relations between families and schools has tended to focus on how parents influence student achievement through a supportive learning environment at home. These studies also have documented a strong connection between higher socioeconomic status (SES) and better performance in school. The present study goes beyond the home to determine the relationship between parent involvement in activities at school and children's academic performance, regardless of the family's social and educational background.

Stevenson and Baker investigate three hypotheses:

1. The higher the mother's educational level, the more parents are involved in school activities
2. The younger the child, the greater the level of parent involvement
3. The more parents are involved in school activities, the better their children do in school.

Research Design

A nationwide random sample of 179 children was selected from the data base of the TIME USE Longitudinal Panel Study. The children were well distributed from ages five to 17, and the mothers had a wide range of educational backgrounds:

Mothers' Educational Levels

High school education or less	35%
Some postsecondary education	42%
College education or more	23%

Parent involvement, defined as being involved in school activities such as the PTO and attending parent-teacher conferences, was rated by teachers from one (low) to five (high). Teacher ratings also assessed the children's school achievement, both in terms of how well children were doing in school and whether they were performing up to their ability.

Findings

First, the authors examined whether the mothers' education and the gender or age of their children are related to the degree of parent involvement in the school. They found that:

"Parental involvement is important to the school performance of both boys and girls, but there are some differences in the strength of this influence across gender. An involved parent has a much stronger impact on the overall school performance of girls than boys."

Parent involvement is a significant predictor: parents who are more involved in school, regardless of their own educational background, have children who perform better in school.

- Parents with more education are more involved in school activities
- Parents of younger children are more likely to be involved in school activities than parents of older children.

When the data for boys and girls are reviewed separately, some interesting differences emerge:

- Parent involvement in girls' education does not vary by the child's age
- For boys, parent involvement is significantly higher while the child is younger.

When they examined the relationship between parent involvement and school performance, the authors found that:

- Parents who are more involved in school activities tend to have children with higher achievement
- When parents participate in school activities, teachers give higher assessments of their children's abilities and potential.

The next level of analysis examined whether parent involvement affects school performance independent of the mother's educational level. The authors found that:

- Parent involvement is a significant predictor: parents who are more involved in school, regardless of their own educational background, have children who perform better in school
- Girls tend to perform better than boys, and older children perform better than younger ones
- Parent involvement has a much stronger impact on the overall academic performance of girls than boys.

Conclusion

Parent involvement mediates almost all the influence of a mother's education on the child's school performance. By itself, the mother's educational level has little effect on her children's success. If they become actively involved in school activities, mothers with less formal education can have as much positive impact as do highly educated mothers.

By itself, the mother's educational level has little effect on her children's success. If they become actively involved in school activities, mothers with less formal education can have as much positive impact as do highly educated mothers.

See also: Baker and Stevenson, Eagle, Reynolds, et al., Ziegler.

Swap, Susan McAllister
Developing Home-School Partnerships: From Concepts to Practice
(*New York: Teachers College Press, Columbia University, 1993*)

SUMMARY: In this book, the author describes four models of home-school relationships and makes a persuasive case for the partnership model, based on a literature review, some exploratory data, and extensive observations. She also provides helpful examples and suggestions for putting the model into practice.

Although partnerships between families and schools produce crucial benefits for children, school-community cultures and district, state and national policies do not support such collaborations. Understanding what Swap calls these "macro-forces" and how they are maintained is an important first step in changing them. The second step is to learn how others have created cultures that do support collaboration. This book attempts to do both.

The Models

The Protective Model: This model, the one in most common practice, is designed to reduce conflict between parents and educators, primarily by separating them. It assumes that parents delegate to the school the responsibility for educating their children, parents hold staff accountable for the results, and educators accept this responsibility. Collaborative problem-solving and routine exchange of information are seen as inappropriate.

The School-To-Home Transmission Model: The goal of this model is to enlist parents in supporting the objectives of the school. If children's achievement is improved when home and school share common expectations and values, then the school should identify the values and practices that contribute to success, and parents should provide these conditions at home.

The Curriculum Enrichment Model: This model is designed to expand the school's curriculum by incorporating contributions of families. Because continuity between home and school encourages children's learning, the curriculum should reflect the children's cultural background. Parents and educators work together to enrich the curriculum and to take advantage of parents' expertise.

The Partnership Model: In this model, parents and educators work together to accomplish the common mission of helping *all* children in the school to achieve success. Accomplishing this mission requires re-thinking the entire school environment, as well as collaboration among parents, community members, and educators. It differs from the other models in that it emphasizes two-way communication, parents' strengths, and joint problem-solving; it also permeates the entire school, rather than being restricted to certain aspects of the curriculum.

"Given the widespread recognition that parent involvement in schools is important, that it is unequivocally related to improvements in children's achievement, and that improvement in children's achievement is urgently needed, it is paradoxical that most schools do not have comprehensive parent involvement programs."

Findings

Swap describes two "partnership" programs that have produced impressive gains in student achievement: James Comer's School Development Program (SDP), and the Accelerated Schools Model. (The SDP is described in the summaries of Comer's research). Swap uses data from the Columbia Park School in Prince George's County, Maryland, where children who once lagged far behind national averages now perform above the 90th percentile in math, and above the 50th percentile in reading.

The Accelerated Schools program, initiated by Henry Levin in California, is designed to accelerate the learning of children who have fallen behind, rather than to treat them as slow learners by giving them simple, repetitive lessons. The program has three main features:

> 1. An accelerated curriculum, using first-hand experience, rich use of language, problem-solving, and higher- order thinking skills.
> 2. Instructional practices that promote active learning, allow students to tutor each other and work together, and encourage teachers to be facilitators, not dictators.
> 3. An organizational model that allows for broad participation of administrators, teachers and parents, building on the strengths of all participants.

In its fourth year of the program, the Daniel Webster School in Redwood City, California, shows significant gains in student achievement compared to other schools in the district. Webster students have increased their average California Test of Basic Skills math scores by 19 percentile points, with all grades performing above grade level. In language, most classes improved at least 10 percentile points. Although these improvements are dramatic, Webster's reading and language scores have not yet reached the national average.

Four Elements of Partnership

The critical elements of partnership between home and school are:

> 1. **Creating two-way communication:** Parents and educators are well informed, negotiate shared expectations for children, and work together to create a school where all learn and feel successful.
> 2. **Enhancing learning at home and at school:** Encouragement of learning is strong and mutually reinforced.
> 3. **Providing mutual support:** Parents support the school in a variety of ways, and the school becomes a key link to health, education and social services for families.
> 4. **Making joint decisions:** Parents and educators are involved in joint problem-solving at every level: child, classroom, school, and district.

Swap devotes a chapter to each element, describing useful strategies in detail from research, case studies, or her own observations.

The elements of partnership are:
- *Two-way communication*
- *Enhancing learning at home and at school*
- *Providing mutual support*
- *Making joint decisions.*

Conclusions

In the final chapter, Swap lays out three paths to partnership and gives useful suggestions for how to embark on them:

Path 1: Establishing a Limited Partnership for Children's Learning. This approach can be used by a single teacher or a team within a school where partnerships are not a high priority. Examples include workshops or summer institutes given by teachers for parents or other teachers.

Path 2: Building a Comprehensive Program: Networks of Mutual Support. This approach offers a variety of school and program options that will appeal to families of different backgrounds. Swap gives examples from two schools that have established a parent center, a home-based Read-Aloud program, a school-parent council, a Big Brothers/Sisters club, and a Models for Success program.

Path 3: Restructuring Schools for Partnership and Student Achievement. This approach attempts to transform the school into a community dedicated to success for all students by embarking on a three- to five-year process. Swap gives examples from the Accelerated Schools program and Effective Schools initiatives.

"Given the widespread recognition that parent involvement in schools is important, that it is unequivocally related to improvements in children's achievement, and that improvement in children's achievement is urgently needed, it is paradoxical that most schools do not have comprehensive parent involvement programs." (p.12)

See also: Becher, Comer, Comer and Haynes, Cummins, Gordon, Leler, Ziegler.

Children who once lagged far behind national averages, now perform above the 90th percentile in math, and above the 50th percentile in reading.

Thompson, Herb
"Quality Education Program/Mississippi: Program Evaluation Panel Report"
Quality Education Project, 639 W. Monterey Road, Corona, CA 91720, 1993

SUMMARY: The Quality Education Program (QEP), designed to increase student success in school by increasing parent involvement, has been implemented in seven school districts in Mississippi. This evaluation report documents both increased parent involvement and significant gains in student academic achievement.

Since its inception in 1982, QEP has been implemented in California, Indiana, and Mississippi. In 1989, the Mississippi State Department of Education selected seven school districts serving a low-income, predominantly African-American population; 27 schools serving 16,000 students in kindergarten through sixth grade then implemented the QEP program. At the time, 87 percent of the parents were not engaged in their children's education and more than 70 percent of the students were below grade level on standardized achievement tests.

Components of the QEP program include:
- **Training of teachers and administrators** in effective school-to-home communication strategies
- **Parent seminars** to provide parenting skills and home support for the child's education
- **Home-school activities**, including Back to School Night, weekly student schoolwork folders, and newsletters for parents
- **School-community efforts**, such as Partnerships in Education, Adopt-a-School programs, and leadership programs that involved community and business leaders with students.

Findings

For purposes of evaluation, the QEP experimental school districts were matched with similar control districts on the basis of poverty, dropout rates, ethnicity, and Mississippi Basic Skills Assessment Program (MS-BSAP) scores. The evaluation was based on:

1. Baseline data for both the experimental and control schools on the number and percent of parents who attend conferences, monitor student homework, and attend school events

2. Surveys, questionnaires, and evaluation instruments administered on a pre-program basis and periodically throughout the duration of the project

3. BSAP scores for each student before the QEP program was implemented compared with student performance two years later.

The statistical analysis revealed that parent involvement in the QEP schools had increased by 65.8 percent over the baseline data and by 45.3

Components of the QEP program include:

♦ *Training teachers and administrators in effective communication skills*

♦ *Parent seminars in home support for education*

♦ *Home-school activities that increase interaction*

♦ *School-community efforts that reach out to community and business leaders.*

percent over the control schools. An "acceptability" survey of staff, parents, and students produced these positive results:

	Yes	No
Is the QEP program helping the child?	88%	12%
Have the child's grades improved?	85%	15%
Does the child study at home?	95%	5%

Between the 1988-89 school year (before the QEP program) and the 1990-91 school year, the QEP districts averaged a 4.8 percent increase in test scores. The control school districts for that same period showed an average increase of only .3 percent. This demonstrates a 4.5 percent advantage of the QEP schools over the control schools. The dropout rate also decreased in the QEP schools, by an average of 5.3 percent over that period, although the control schools experienced a similar decline.

Conclusions

"The continuing MS-QEP program will contribute to long-term student success in school as evidenced in positive trend gains in academic achievement scores over the baseline data for experimental schools and the data for control schools." (p. 9)

See also: Beane, Comer and Haynes, Simich-Dudgeon.

Between the 1988-89 school year (before the QEP program) and the 1990-91 school year the QEP districts averaged a 4.8 percent increase in test scores. The control school districts for that same period showed an average increase of only .3 percent.

Tizard, J., W.N. Schofield, and Jenny Hewison   *EJ264 773*
"Collaboration Between Teachers and Parents in Assisting Children's Reading"
British Journal of Educational Psychology, *Vol.52, Part 1, pp.1-11, 1982*

SUMMARY: **The authors find that elementary-grade children who practice reading at home with parents make highly significant gains in reading achievement at school, in comparison with control group students and children who practiced at school with teachers.**

All children in the middle-infant (five-six years old), top infant, first-year junior, and second-year junior classes at six schools in a disadvantaged working-class area of London were studied over the course of two years. The 1900 students involved were divided into three comparable groups chosen at random.

Children in the experimental group read aloud to their parents two to four times a week, from books sent home with them from school; from time to time, parents received encouragement or tips on "good practice" from their children's teachers. A control group received no routine of extra reading time beyond school instruction. A third group received extra reading help about twice a week at school, from a special teacher hired for the project; this teacher not only listened to the students read (duplicating the at-home experiment), but offered additional assistance in all aspects of the teaching of reading.

Students from the four grades were tested using a wide variety of reading achievement tests geared to measure their progress from one grade level to the next. The tests were administered before the interventions began, and then at the conclusion of the next three school years-- that is, until the first middle-infant students had become the last second-year juniors.

Findings

The results show "highly significant improvement by children who received extra practice at home in comparison with control groups, but not comparable improvement by children who received extra help at school. The gains were made consistently by children of all ability levels." (p.1) For the experimental group, the improvement in reading scores brought their average level of achievement up to the national standard, whereas before the intervention, over 80 percent were reading below age level. "Thus the figure of around 50 percent (performing at age level) observed in the two parent involvement groups represents an improvement in standards over that usually achieved by even the most successful school in the sample." (p.10)

"The results show highly significant improvement by children who received extra practice at home in comparison with control groups, but not comparable improvement by children who received extra help at school. The gains were made consistently by children of all ability levels."

Conclusion

The researchers feel the study verifies earlier research indicating gains in achievement by students whose parents helped them read at home, and demonstrates the broad power of parental involvement as being more effective even than extra-curricular involvement of teachers.

See also: Leler, Sattes, Toomey.

"The figure of around 50 percent (performing at age level) observed in the two parent involvement groups represents an improvement in standards over that usually achieved by even the most successful school in the sample."

The programs offering home visits were more successful in involving disadvantaged parents than were programs requiring parents to visit the school, but the programs requiring parents to visit the school produced higher gains in reading competence.

"The dynamics of 'normal' home-school relations converted a home-visit type of program into a 'volunteer' type of program in which especial benefits, or at least a high profile, goes to those families with parents who regularly visit the school."

Toomey, Derek   ED 269 495
"Home-School Relations and Inequality in Education"
School of Education, La Trobe University, Melbourne Australia. Address given
to a Conference on Education and the Family, Brigham Young University,
February 1986

SUMMARY: A study of low-income schools in the state of Victoria, Australia, found that programs to encourage parent involvement in the development of young children's reading skills were successful in producing greater reading competence, especially for parents who had a high level of contact with the school.

In this retrospective review of a series of studies he conducted between 1982 and 1985, the author found that while programs to increase parent involvement in reading competence have positive effects, "the normal operation of home-school relations may actually increase educational inequality."

The model studied exhibited two variations on a form of parent participation: Parents are asked to support their children's education with activities in the home and:

1. Are invited to visit the school to receive information and advice, or
2. Are visited at home and given information and encouragement.

Findings

The programs offering home visits were more successful in involving disadvantaged parents than were programs requiring parents to visit the school, but the programs requiring parents to visit the school produced higher gains in reading competence. The author speculates that this discrepancy is caused by bias: teachers favor parents who are willing to come to school, and the parents who come to school are more self-confident and committed to the program. A cycle of positive reinforcement leads to gains for those children whose parents come to school and shuts out families who are more comfortable at home.

Toomey presents an interesting typology of low-income parents:

		Parents help child's reading	
		Yes	**No**
Parents readily	**Yes**	Enthusiasts	Ambiguous
visit school	**No**	Silent Majority	Uninvolved

The experience of the projects studied is that "the dynamics of 'normal' home-school relations converted a home-visit type of program into a 'volunteer' type of program in which especial benefits, or at least a high profile, goes to those families with parents who regularly visit the school."

Conclusion

While the parents who did receive home visits said they increased their self-confidence in helping with their children's education and in dealing with the school, they were also discouraged by the "in-group" of parents who were based at the school. Home visits became less frequent as the ease of working with parents at school increased, and the final result was that the school neglected the "silent majority" for the "enthusiasts."

See also: Lareau, Leler, Tizard et al.

While the parents who did receive home visits said they increased their self-confidence in helping with their children's education and in dealing with the school, they were also discouraged by the "in-group" of parents who were based at the school.

Wagenaar, Theodore C.   *ED 146 111*
"School Achievement Level Vis-a-Vis Community Involvement and Support:
An Empirical Assessment"
Ohio State University, Columbus, Hershon Center. Paper presented at the
Annual Meeting of the American Sociological Association, September 1977

SUMMARY: This study of the public elementary schools in a large midwestern city finds that schools that are more open to parent and community involvement have higher levels of student achievement, and that more closed schools have lower achievement levels and less community support.

Wagenaar gathered data from 135 elementary schools to determine the relationship between levels of community involvement and support, and the average reading and math test scores for each school. Controlling for SES (socioeconomic status), to factor out any effects of class bias, and using average figures for each school to test the effect on the entire school's performance rather than on that of individual students, the data were correlated to determine the relationship between types of community support and involvement, and levels of student achievement.

"Community involvement and support" was measured according to 29 separate items, or definitions, that covered fund raising and political support by active community groups, opportunities for parents to participate in school activities and meet with teachers, numbers of parents and citizens who participate in school meetings and functions, percentage of voters who participated in last school bond issue, number of times community groups use school facilities, number of contacts between principal or teachers and parents at school and at home, and the role of citizens in school policy decisions, such as selecting curricula, hiring teachers, setting discipline procedures, and allocating more budget.

Findings

Most significantly related to achievement were the measures of community group support and fund raising, attending school meetings, and number of school functions. Also related was the number of times community groups use school facilities. Somewhat less related, but still significant, were discussion opportunities and school-parent contact. Neither of the two citizen participation-in-policy factors was found to be related to achievement.

"In sum. . .analysis indicates a generally positive relationship between school achievement level and such factors as behavioral involvement and support, use of school facilities, and an open communications atmosphere. But actual participation in decision-making is apparently unrelated to achievement. (p.13)

"By improving the number, types, and levels of interaction, by improving the communication between school and community, and by utilizing community resources, it is suggested that schools may become more effective in the future."

Conclusion

The author speculates that more open school systems are more effective, and that a supportive and involved environment is more beneficial than a power-wielding environment. "By improving the number, types, and levels of interaction, by improving the communication between school and community, and by utilizing community resources, it is suggested that schools may become more effective in the future." (p.18)

See also: Chavkin, Coleman and Hoffer, McDill, Phillips.

The positive relationships exists in spite of controls for school socioeconomic status and several structural factors.

Walberg, Herbert J.
"Families as Partners in Educational Productivity"
Phi Delta Kappan, *February 1984, pp.397-400*

SUMMARY: In this article summarizing findings from over 2500 studies on learning, Walberg concludes that an academically stimulating home environment is one of eight chief determinants of learning; and from 29 recent studies he concludes that the home learning environment has an effect on achievement that is three times as large as family socio-economic status (SES).

The *"Matthew effect:"* those who are well-prepared gain abundantly, while those who have not fall further and further behind.

Economists studying the development of human resources confirm a biblical text, one Walberg calls the "Matthew effect:" those who are well-prepared gain abundantly, while those who have not fall further and further behind. In short, the rich get richer and the poor get poorer. "Stimulating educative experiences in families and schools predicted adult knowledge much more decisively than did adult motivation and effort. Those who began well gained knowledge at faster rates throughout their adult lives." (p.398)

Findings

Walberg extracted the major findings from 2,575 empirical studies on academic learning to identify eight chief determinants of cognitive, affective, and behavioral learning.

Four are direct determinants:

- Student ability
- Student motivation
- Quality of instruction
- Amount of instruction

Four are indirect or supportive determinants:

"Educators, families and students would do well to insure that more of youngsters' discretionary time is spent on academic study and other constructive pursuits."

- Psychological climate of the classroom
- Academically stimulating home environment
- Peer group with academic goals and activities
- Minimum exposure to low-grade television

Because children spend so much time at home or under the control of their parents, altering home conditions and the relations between home and school should product large effects on learning. Studies on homework show that "homework produces uniformly positive effects on the factual, conceptual, critical, and attitudinal aspects of learning." (p.399)

A group of 29 controlled studies done in the past decade showed significant improvements for students whose families participated in programs designed to improve the learning environment of the home. From these studies, Walberg identifies a "curriculum of the home," which predicts academic learning twice as well as the socioeconomic status of families. This curriculum includes:

- Informed parent-child conversations about everyday events
- Encouragement and discussion of leisure reading
- Monitoring and joint analysis of televiewing
- Deferral of immediate gratification to achieve long-range goals
- Expressions of affection
- Interest in children's academic and personal growth

Conclusions

"Educators, families and students would do well to insure that more of youngsters' discretionary time is spent on academic study and other constructive pursuits." (p.399) Although parents and teachers may not always agree on what roles are most appropriate for parents to play, all agree that more parent involvement than now exists would be preferable. "Moreover, the nation can ill afford to let any potentially helpful group remain a silent partner in solving the national crisis in productivity." (p.400)

See also: Clark (1990, 1993), Reynolds, Walberg et al.

The "curriculum of the home":
- *Informed parent-child conversations*
- *Encouragement of leisure reading*
- *Limits on television-watching*
- *Focus on long-range goals*
- *Expressions of affection*
- *Interest in children's growth.*

*When parents do
these things at
home, children do
better at school:
1. Provide a
special place for
study
2. Encourage the
child daily by
discussion
3. Attend to the
student's progress
in school
4.Compliment the
child on any gains
5. Cooperate with
the teacher.*

Walberg, H. J., R. E. Bole, and H. C. Waxman
"School-Based Family Socialization and Reading Achievement in the Inner-City"
Psychology in the Schools, *Vol.17, 1980, pp.509-514*

SUMMARY: Elementary school students in grades one to six, whose parents and teachers responded to a city-wide program to improve academic support in the home, gained .5 to .6 grade equivalents in reading comprehension over students less intensively involved.

In response to a survey in which parents asked for more home-school cooperation and community activities centered around education, joint parent-staff committees in Chicago initiated a program to help parents encourage their children at home. A contract signed by the superintendent, principal, teacher, parents, and the student stipulated that parents would:

1. Provide a special place in the home for study
2. Encourage the child daily by discussion
3. Attend to the student's progress in school and compliment the child on any gains
4. Cooperate with the teacher in providing these things properly.

A booklet of "school policies and academic activities" was distributed to 650 parents at an open house, as well as at parent-teacher visits and book fairs. More than 99 percent of the students in 41 classes (826 in grades one to six) held such contracts signed by all parties. After one school year in the program, the Iowa Test of Basic Skills (ITBS) was administered to all the children.

Findings

Two variables accounted for nearly all the reliable variance in post-test scores: program intensity and prior reading comprehension score on the ITBS. Program intensity was determined by the rating a student's teacher received from the school principal as intensive, or not intensive, in the use of parent-involvement. ITBS scores from the previous year served as the pre-test standardized reference.

After a year in the program, "classes whose parents were intensively involved in the program gained an estimated 1.1 grade equivalents (or a little more than one year); classes whose parents were less intensively involved gained only .5 grade equivalents (or only about half year).

Conclusion

"Effective child-centered and home-based programs require as many as three professionals or paraprofessionals for groups of 20 to 25 young children, extensive recruiting, and costs of up to $5,000 per child. Parent programs initiated in the schools may prove to be as effective, less costly, and capable of sustaining reasonable gains throughout the elementary school years." (p.514)

See also: Clark (1990, 1993), Dauber and Epstein, Epstein.

"Classes whose parents were intensively involved in the program gained an estimated 1.1 grade equivalents (or a little more than one year); classes whose parents were less intensively involved gained only .5 grade equivalents (or only about half year)."

White, Karl R., Matthew J. Taylor, and Vanessa D. Moss
"Does Research Support Claims About the Benefits of Involving Parents in Early Intervention Programs?"
Review of Educational Research, *Vol.62, No.1, Spring 1992, pp.91-125*

SUMMARY: This analysis of 193 studies of programs for disadvantaged and handicapped children whose parents were trained to teach their preschoolers developmental skills, suggests that because so few studies were well-designed, the evidence that such involvement benefits the children is not convincing.

> *The authors do not contend that parent involvement makes no difference, but find that most studies they examined present contradictory findings or are methodologically flawed.*

> *"Many good ideas fail to produce expected results because of poor implementation, not because the concept is wrong."*

Of the more than 100 books, articles, papers, reports, and studies reviewed for this annotated bibliography, only this one review questions the finding that parent involvement results in improved student achievement. The authors do *not* contend that parent involvement makes no difference, but find that most studies they examined present contradictory findings or are methodologically flawed.

This paper selected six widely cited reviews of early intervention programs for close scrutiny (two are summarized elsewhere in this book, see Bronfenbrenner and Lazar). All six concluded that early intervention programs will be more effective if they involve parents. White, Taylor and Moss then analyzed each study cited in these six reviews, as well as a data base from other related studies, to determine whether they support the claim that parent involvement improves children's performance. To be considered reliable, the studies had to involve a direct test of whether the intervention is more effective when parents are involved than when they are not, and to meet the following rigorous standards for validity:

- subjects were randomly assigned to two groups, and drawn from a stratified sample
- the two groups were comparable in terms of demographics and family functioning
- families were interviewed to determine special circumstances that might compromise the comparability of the two groups
- the alternative interventions were described in detail and verified for proper implementation
- assessments were done in a neutral location by trained testers
- the groups remained intact from pre-test to post-test.

All the studies reviewed looked at early intervention programs for children who are handicapped, disadvantaged, or at risk. Although White et al. identify four types of parent involvement in such programs, they focus on only one in their analysis. This type they term "parents as intervenors," defined as "parent teaches developmental skills (e.g. motor, language, self-help) to the child."

Findings

Of the 20 studies covered in the six reviews, the authors determined that only three, two of which were judged to have low validity, involved a direct test. Only one of these found a positive effect on the children. Three more studies compared intervention programs that were similar, but not the same, so that differences in achievement might be attributed to other components. These findings were mixed. Nine studies compared children in interventions that have parent involvement with children who received no intervention, and the remaining five studies looked at programs that did not substantially involve parents.

For the 173 additional studies in the data base, the authors performed a number of statistical analyses depending upon the type of study (direct versus indirect effects), type of program (center-based or home-based), and type of child served (handicapped or disadvantaged). Again, the authors found few studies that met the validity criteria and that documented direct, statistically significant benefits for children whose parents were involved, compared with children whose parents were not involved.

"In summary, we found no evidence of larger effect sizes for intervention versus no-intervention studies which involved parents versus similar studies which did not involve parents. Admittedly, the potential for confounding variables to obscure true relationships in a data set of this nature is substantial. Furthermore, as shown by the data reported...most of these studies have focused primarily or even exclusively on using parents as intervenors instead of involving them in other ways. Thus, it would be inappropriate to conclude, based on these data, that parent involvement in early intervention is not beneficial. Just as important, however, is the fact that no information exists in this admittedly indirect type of evidence to argue that parent involvement in early intervention will lead to any of the benefits that are often claimed." (p.109)

The authors offer three possible explanations for their findings:
- The focus on using parents primarily as supplemental intervenors may be the wrong approach
- Little research has verified that the program was well implemented or that parents participated to the desired degree
- Not enough attention has been given to the effects of parent involvement activities on parents and family members.

Conclusion

The authors conclude that "claims that parent involvement in early intervention leads to benefits...are without foundation and should be disregarded until such time as defensible research is available to support such a position." (p.118)

See also: Bronfenbrenner, Goodson and Hess, Gotts, Guinagh and Gordon, Lazar, Mowry, Pfannensteil, Radin, Schweinhart and Weikart.

"No information exists in this admittedly indirect type of evidence to argue that parent involvement in early intervention will lead to any of the benefits that are often claimed."

"The fact that existing laws mandate the involvement of parents in early intervention programs for handicapped and at-risk children emphasizes the need to continue to examine what types of parent involvement are most beneficial for children and families."(p. 120)

Children from mainstream Appalachian and Chinese-American families are successful because the middle-class values and models of learning promoted at home are compatible with those at school.

"While children from low-achieving groups can benefit from opportunities to acquire some of the experiences, strategies, and outlooks that are expected in school, they gain little if these programs cause their parents to lose confidence in their child-rearing abilities."

Wong Fillmore, Lily
"Now or Later? Issues Related to the Early Education of Minority-Group Children"
In Early Childhood and Family Education: Analysis and Recommendations of the Council of Chief State School Officers, *New York: Harcourt Brace Jovanovich, 1990, pp.122-145*

SUMMARY: This article reviews research on child-rearing practices in different cultural, racial, and language minority families, and why they may not match the preparation children need for American schools. The author also recommends ways that early-education programs can help such children adjust to school without damage to their family relationships.

The disparity in academic performance among children from different minority groups has prompted much research. Although some families fail to create an adequate home environment, most parents nurture and love their children, and cannot be characterized as deficient. The type of socialization, child-rearing, and skill development natural in certain cultural groups, however, appears not to match the background children need to be successful in mainstream American public schools.

Wong Fillmore describes the cultural backgrounds of five different racial and ethnic groups, drawing from observational and ethnographic research, and discusses how school performance is affected by the child-rearing practices in the home.

Findings

One researcher looked at the cultural background of three types of rural Appalachian families: mainstream (middle class), working-class Whites, and working-class Blacks. Parents in mainstream families view babies as "separate, knowing individuals," and talk to them as if they could answer. As soon as they talk, children are encouraged to ask questions and are praised for making up stories and talking about books. These children experience years of literacy preparation before they enter school. Wong Fillmore describes the relationship between home and school as a "seamless splice." (p.124)

In White working-class families, parents tend not to converse with their infants and toddlers; instead, they teach their children what they should think and know. These constraints on communication and learning teach children that there are limits on what they need to understand or to question. When the children enter school they tend to be passive learners, unprepared to be the source of information. They do well in school until they have to take an active role in learning, at which point they begin to lose ground.

In contrast, Black working-class parents tend to communicate with babies in non-verbal ways, surrounding them with loving human contact but rarely speaking to them directly. Children learn by imitating adults, at their own pace. Adults tend not to ask questions, but delight in verbal virtuosity and storytelling. When ready to join in the adult talk, children must be assertive. At school, this assertiveness may be considered disrespectful, and the children have difficulty answering questions directed to them and dealing with desk-bound activities.

Another researcher studied child-rearing in Chinese-American families. From the very beginning, parents train their children to conform to adult expectations, emphasizing morality, good manners, respect for elders, and humility. Children are supervised closely, trained to do things well, and told that they can do anything they choose if they put enough effort into it. Even though Chinese-American children often have little experience with books or reading, they do well in school, drawing on the "astounding" work habits and skills developed at home.

A group of three researchers have observed Mexican-American and other Latino youngsters. In these families, parents believe their children are born with distinct characteristics; parents guide, but do not control. Although their beliefs may seem fatalistic, parents are active in shaping their children's character. Children are respectful, know the virtue and value of work, and are patient, responsible and cooperative. Still, they do not prosper in American schools.

Conclusions

Wong Fillmore concludes that children from mainstream Appalachian and Chinese-American families are successful because the middle-class values and models of learning promoted at home are compatible with those at school. Working-class Black and White children and Mexican-Americans tend not to perform well because their socialization has emphasized social behavior, not literacy; they learn by observation and imitation, not by direct instruction or coaching; and their parents have encouraged an individual pace of development rather than keeping up with other children.

As a result, many early-childhood programs are designed to "better socialize" children so that they are more like the mainstream. Wong Fillmore responds bluntly:

"More harm than good can come from programs that are founded on such beliefs. While children from low-achieving groups can benefit from opportunities to acquire some of the experiences, strategies, and outlooks that are expected in school, they gain little if these programs cause their parents to lose confidence in their child-rearing abilities. Consider the message they convey to parents: *You are inadequate; you are doing a poor job preparing your children for school; there is something wrong with your culture.* Such messages cannot be good for parents--or for their children." (p. 134)

Wong Fillmore believes that the more securely children are anchored in their primary culture the better their chances to adjust successfully to

"The problem lies not in a lack of preparation for learning but instead in the mismatch between the preparation provided by the home and that which is expected by the school. What is needed are programs that build on the children's home experiences while providing some of the experiences needed for school."

"There can be no more powerful argument in favour of parental involvement in their children's schooling than the fact that it is strongly and positively associated with children's achievement in school and attitude toward learning."

new environments. The major objectives of early childhood programs should be to encourage young children to develop curiosity, to explore environments, and to develop social relationships, rather than to promote academic learning.

See also: Caplan et al., Comer, Cummins, Reynolds, Scott-Jones (1987), Simich-Dudgeon, Ziegler.

Ziegler, Suzanne   ED 304 234
"The Effects of Parent Involvement on Children's Achievement:
The Significance of Home/School Links"
Toronto Board of Education, Ontario, Canada, October 1987

SUMMARY: This report reviews research and program evaluations that document the positive effects of parent involvement at home and at school. It also discusses the whys and hows of connecting parents and schools, and suggests techniques for overcoming barriers and building commitment to parent-school partnerships.

This report was prepared for the Toronto Board of Education to help develop a policy on home/school relations. Not only does Ziegler review the research literature on the impact of parent involvement, she also provides many program examples, along with evaluation data, from Canada, England and the United States.

Ziegler is clearly convinced that parent involvement in children's schooling is strongly related to academic achievement and constructive attitudes toward learning. She identifies two critical messages from the research:

- The gap in school achievement between working-class and middle-class children is more effectively explained by differing patterns of child-parent and parent-school interaction than it is by characteristics of socioeconomic status (SES).
- School personnel can intervene positively and effectively to show parents how to help their children be successful. The attitudes and behavior of parents who have felt powerless and excluded *can* be changed. Aggressive outreach techniques may be necessary to establish communication with ethnic, racial, and language-minority families.

Findings on Parent Involvement at Home

School-related activities carried out by parents at home strongly influence children's long-term academic success at all ages.

Preschool Level: Several longitudinal studies demonstrate long-lasting benefits to children who participated in preschool programs that include home visits and/or involve parents at school. Benefits include higher achievement, better attendance, lower drop-out rates, improved high school completion rates, and higher college/university admissions.

Elementary Level: Parent participation in reading and literacy programs can result in higher student achievement, even with parents of varied language background and low literacy skills.

Middle and High School Level: Students whose parents are aware of what their children are studying at school, who are in regular communication with their teachers, and who help to reinforce schoolwork, show higher achievement all the way through secondary school.

School personnel can intervene positively and effectively to show parents how to help their children be successful. The attitudes and behavior of parents who have felt powerless and excluded can be changed.

It is important to recognize that the presence of parents in the school not only provides more adults to teach reading or offer help and support to children, but also transforms the culture of the school."

Findings on Parent Involvement at School

Parent involvement in education is equally powerful whether the involvement occurs at home or at school. "It is important to recognize that the presence of parents in the school not only provides more adults to teach reading or offer help and support to children, but also transforms the *culture* of the school." (p.34) Mothers report that many problems in school disappear when their children see an alliance between mother and teacher, and when mothers can help teachers be more responsive to their children.

Although there is little research on positive effects on student achievement from parent involvement in governance, this review concludes that significant gains for students occur when the governance role is "made truly integral to a school's central policy-making, and when a school has a very defined and significant decision-making focus and structure." (p.41)

Findings on Connecting Parents and Schools

A strong connection between parents and teachers signifies to the child a "goal consensus," that parent and teacher expectations are similar, and that school and home will both be supportive. Thus families and school are seen as overlapping rather than separate spheres of influence.

Ziegler reviews the work of a number of researchers to suggest characteristics of effective parent-involvement programs. These include clear goals and objectives, parent training, appropriate materials, two-way communication, and monitoring of progress.

Conclusion

"The influence of the home on children's success at school is profound. Whether indirectly, as models, or directly, as readers, audience, or homework helpers, parents' learning-related and school-related activities at home are a very strong influence on children's long-term academic success." (p.5)

See also: Cummins, Epstein, Sattes, Swap, Toomey.

Significant gains for students occur when the governance role is "made truly integral to a school's central policy-making, and when a school has a very defined and significant decision-making focus and structure."

Epilogue

This report is the final publication of the National Committee for Citizens in Education. It caps a long and distinguished series of handbooks, reports, manuals, brochures, and action guides -- a virtual library aimed at materially improving the relationship between families and schools.

After its first report, "Parents, Children and School Records," which led to the enactment of the Family Educational Rights and Privacy Act in 1974, NCCE developed a series of cards and pocket-sized handbooks summarizing parents' rights and dealing with critical issues such as parents' organizing, school closings, collective bargaining, and school violence. Years of experience with the Help Line, over which the staff gave advice and counsel to thousands of parents, teachers, students, and citizens, gave us ideas for rack-sized paperbacks such as *Parents Schools and the Law, How to Run a School Board Campaign -- and Win,* and *The School Budget: It's Your Money, It's Your Business.* To respond quickly to the questions asked most often, we developed the Information for Parents Series, 12 brochures in English and Spanish on key topics.

Along the way, we noticed that many of our callers and book-buyers were educators -- teachers and administrators also needed help in building strong relationships between schools and families. This led to *Beyond the Bake Sale: An Educator's Guide to Working with Parents,* the Evidence series, and training manuals on family and community involvement in school based management.

In addition to parent advocacy, NCCE has always had a strong interest in those the schools have not served well. *Helping Dreams Survive* tells the story of NCCE's project to work with low-income African-American families whose middle-school children were at risk of dropping out. *Beyond Barriers* documents a related project with Hispanic families.

For readers of *A New Generation of Evidence* who want to take action, we especially recommend *Taking Stock: The Inventory of Family, School and Community Partnerships for Student Achievement* as a first step in assessing the current relationship.

In these past 20 years, the atmosphere has become far more friendly to the idea that schools should collaborate with families. We would like to think that NCCE's work has made a major contribution to that change, not only from the now wide acceptance of the evidence that involving parents improves student achievement, but also from the information and tools we have developed to build the collaborations needed to do the job. We wish you well.

NCCE publications will continue to be available through the Center for Law and Education.

197 Friend St., 9th Floor
Boston, MA 02114
and
1875 Connecticut Ave., NW, Suite 510
Washington, D.C. 20009

About the Editors and Illustrator

Anne T. Henderson   Anne has been a consultant to the National Committee for Citizens in Education since 1977, the year her daughter Amy-Louise was born. In addition to representing the interests of public school families before federal policymakers, she has managed several projects, such as community involvement in school-based improvement and urban middle school restructuring, and represented NCCE on the National Coalition for Parent Involvement in Education. Aside from editing *The Evidence Grows* and *The Evidence Continues to Grow*, she is also co-author of *Taking Stock: The Inventory of Family, School and Community Support for Student Achievement*, *The Middle School Years: A Parent's Handbook*, and *Beyond the Bake Sale*. She is currently collaborating on a set of materials to be entitled "Supporting our Kids: A Family-School-Community Campaign."

Nancy Berla   Nancy served as director of NCCE's information clearinghouse from 1983 until 1991, creating an invaluable resource for parents and citizens, and overseeing the 800-NETWORK Help Line. She has also coauthored several books on parent involvement, most recently *Innovations in Parent and Family Involvement* (1993), with William Rioux, also *Taking Stock* (with Jocelyn Garlington) and *The Middle School Years* (with Bill Kerewsky). In addition, she developed the Information for Parents Series on topics such as parents' rights, corporal punishment, school records, and individual education plans. She is now a writer and consultant.

Bill Harris   A native of Virginia, Mr. Harris has taught art from the elementary to the university level. He currently teaches at Old Dominion University in Norfolk. "The neighborhood themes in my work arise from my own childhood remembrances. Families in my neighborhood stayed together through rough and good times. I was fortunate to have both a father and mother at home to love me. My work pays homage to the men (especially my dad) who have stayed with their families to lead us children into adulthood."

Index